FAMOUS REGIMENTS

The Highland Light Infantry

FAMOUS REGIMENTS

Edited by
Lt.-General Sir Brian Horrocks

The Highland Light Infantry

(The 71st **H.L.I** and 74th **Highlanders**)

by L. B. Oatts

Leo Cooper Ltd., London

PRINTED IN GREAT BRITAIN
BY EBENEZER BAYLIS AND SON, LTD.
THE TRINITY PRESS, WORCESTER, AND LONDON

by Lt.-General Sir Brian Horrocks

IT IS ALWAYS sad when old friends depart. In the last few years many famous old regiments have disappeared, merged into larger formations.

I suppose this is inevitable; strategy and tactics are always changing, forcing the structure of the Army to change too. But the memories of the past still linger in minds now trained to great technical proficiency and surrounded by sophisticated equipment. Nevertheless the disappearance of these well-known names as separate units marks the end of a military epoch; but we must never forget that, throughout the years, each of these regiments has carved for itself a special niche in British History. The qualities of the British character, both good and bad, which helped England to her important position in the world can be seen at work in the regiments of the old Army. To see why these regiments succeeded under Marlborough and Wellington yet failed in the American War of Independence should help us in assessing the past.

Though many Battle Honours were won during historic campaigns, the greatest contribution which our Regiments have made to the British Empire is rarely mentioned: this has surely been the protection they have afforded to those indomitable British merchants, who in search of fresh markets spread our influence all over the world. For some of these this involved spending many years in stinking garrisons overseas where their casualties from disease were often far greater than those suffered on active service.

The main strength of our military system has always lain

in the fact that regimental roots were planted deep into the British countryside in the shape of the Territorial Army whose battalions are also subject to the cold winds of change. This ensured the closest possible link between civilian and military worlds, and built up a unique County and family *esprit de corps* which exists in no other Army in the World. A Cockney regiment, a West Country regiment and a Highland regiment differed from each other greatly, though they fought side by side in scores of battles. In spite of miserable conditions and savage discipline, a man often felt he belonged within the regiment—he shared the background and the hopes of his fellows. That was a great comfort for a soldier. Many times, at Old Comrades' gatherings, some old soldier has come up to me and said, referring to one of the World Wars, 'They were good times, Sir, weren't they?'

They were not good times at all. They were horrible times; but what these men remember and now miss was the comradeship and *esprit de corps* of the old regular regiments. These regiments, which bound men together and helped them through the pain and fear of war, deserve to be recalled.

Regimental histories are usually terribly dull, as the authors are forced to record the smallest operation and include as many names as possible. In this series we have something new. Freed from the tyranny of minute detail, the authors have sought to capture that subtle quarry, the regimental spirit. The history of each regiment is a story of a type of British life now fading away. These stories illuminate the past, and should help us to think more clearly about the military future.

The Highland Light Infantry

A SPECIAL INTRODUCTION

by Lt.-General Sir Brian Horrocks

SINCE THEY were first formed as Lord Macleod's Highlanders in 1777, the H.L.I. have fought with great distinction all over the world. I do not believe any other can claim to have taken part in every major campaign fought by the British Army, and Colonel Oatts has shown great skill in successfully condensing the record of so much hard fighting into this small book.

Every unit in the British Army has its own particular battle honour of which it is especially proud, and which it celebrates annually. None is more worthy than the Battle of Assaye, commemorated by the H.L.I. and fought on September 23, 1803, which is here vividly described. With only about 6,000 men, less than half of whom were British, the future Duke of Wellington, then Major-General Arthur Wellesley, overcame 60,000 Mahrattas, trained and led by European officers, mostly French. When they began to give way at last, Wellesley ordered a general advance, and observing that the 74th Highlanders (2nd H.L.I.) on the right flank had not complied, rode over to find that out of seventeen officers and 500 men, only about forty were still on their feet, led by the Quartermaster, who had run forward from the baggage-train to take command when he saw that all the officers had fallen. Although practically wiped-out, the 74th had withstood all attempts by the enemy to break the right flank, by turning all their guns upon it and making repeated massed cavalry charges. No wonder that the Iron Duke, who was not given to compliments, alluded to them as 'my fighting regiment', and when they joined him in Portugal on March 16, 1810, said to their C.O., 'if the 74th fight as well in the Peninsula as they did in India, y'ought to be damned proud of 'em, by God!'

In the Peninsular War the 71st (1st H.L.I.) and 74th took part in almost all Wellington's victories. The 74th were in the 3rd. or 'Fighting Division', commanded by the famous Picton, whose bravery was only matched by his picturesque language. It was he who, though seriously wounded, led them against the massive walls of the Castle of Badajoz. Some years ago, I stood on the very spot where this attack was launched, and it seemed incredible, that in the face of considerable opposition, these walls could possibly have been scaled at all.

Seventeen H.L.I. battalions fought in the 1914-18 War, and took part in sixty-four major engagements. Time after time they were almost completely wiped-out, yet they always 'came again.' I wonder if any other regiment can claim to have fought in France, Belgium, the Dardanelles, Egypt, Palestine and Mesopotamia.

In March, 1945, during the final stage of the last war, seven battalions of the regiment, including their allied regiment, the H.L.I. of Canada, were serving at one time in my Corps: the 1st H.L.I. in the 53rd Division, the 2nd Glasgow Highlanders and 10th H.L.I. in the 15th (Scottish) Division and the famous 157th (H.L.I.) Brigade, consisting of the 5th and 6th H.L.I. and 1st Glasgow Highlanders, in the 52nd (Lowland) Division. It was this Brigade which took a prominent part in the capture of Bremen. All these battalions fought extremely well. When I once remarked on the uniformly high fighting qualities of so many battalions from the same regiment, one of their most distinguished commanders answered, with a twinkle in his eye, 'you must remember, General, that they come from Glasgow and are mainly of both Scots and Irish descent. They are prepared to fight anyone, anywhere and at any time—so when the fighting is legalized, so to speak, as in war, they are in their element and you could not wish for better troops; but in peacetime or in some boring foreign station, they need first-class leaders, or you really are in for trouble.'

Regarding their peacetime activities, I can remember only their formidable reputation on the football field, but bearing in mind the fact that the primary object of any Army is to fight, I reckon that Glasgow can be extremely proud of her very own regiment.

Acknowledgements

The author and publishers would like to thank Brigadier E. J. Montgomery, C.B., C.B.E., late of the H.L.I. who read the manuscript and made helpful suggestions. Thanks are also due to Captain Archie Wilson of the Regimental Headquarters, Royal Highland Fusiliers who has been so helpful throughout the preparation of this book.

Chapter

I

Early Adventures

THE Highland Light Infantry was raised in 1777 by John Mackenzie, Lord Macleod, elder son of the Earl of Cromartie. After the forfeiture of his family's estates for its part in the 1745 rebellion, Macleod had entered the service of the King of Sweden, in which he had risen to Lieutenant-General. At least fifteen of the original officers were Mackenzies, several of whom had served in the Swedish or Dutch armies; although George Mackenzie, Macleod's brother, was transferred from the Black Watch.

The original composition of the regiment was 840 Highlanders, recruited from the Mackenzie country, 240 Lowlanders from Glasgow, and thirty-four English and Irish. Its uniform was a scarlet jacket with buff facings, a feather bonnet, and the *breacan-an-fheilidh* or belted plaid of six ells of double-width tartan. The tartan was the dark 'Government Issue', as worn by the Black Watch, but shortly after the regiment had been raised, red and buff stripes were added; the buff stripes being later changed to white. This tartan; a green background with red and white stripes, has ever after been known as the Mackenzie tartan, although whether it is the same as that originally worn by the Clan Mackenzie is doubtful.

The regiment was first known as Lord Macleod's Highlanders, and was numbered the 73rd. Later, following the disbandment of the 'Old 71st', or Fraser's Highlanders, its number was changed from 73rd to 71st, and it became the next senior Highland Regiment to the Black Watch.

Macleod's Highlanders mustered at Elgin in 1778, and

The 71st Highlanders on the march.

were passed fit for service. At the same time a second battalion was raised under George Mackenzie. Command of the 1st battalion then passed to Duncan Macpherson of Cluny, who had arrived from Fraser's Highlanders. He was known in the Highlands as 'Duncan of the Kiln', owing to the fact that the dangers and stresses of the '45 rebellion had obliged his mother to give birth to him secretly in a lime-kiln.

Times were bad. The mishandling of the revolt in the American colonies had led to Burgoyne's surrender at Saratoga in 1777, and in the following year Great Britain was at war with both France and Spain; in fear of invasion and with all her overseas possessions in danger. There was thus no chance of Macleod's Highlanders being kept idle. In January 1779, the 1st battalion sailed for India to fight Haidar Ali in Mysore and the Carnatic, and in November the 2nd battalion sailed for Gibraltar, which was being besieged by Spain. It arrived at the Rock on January 18, 1780, just two days before the 1st battalion reached Madras.

The voyage to Gibraltar was far from dull. The transports carrying the 2nd battalion were accompanied by a large fleet of merchantmen with supplies for the beleagured garrison, and escorted by twenty-seven sail of the line and nine frigates, commanded by Admiral Sir George Rodney. A large convoy of Spanish merchantmen and warships was encountered on January 8, which was chased by Rodney who captured the lot. He sent them home under prize crews, which left his ships so short-handed that he ordered the Highlanders on board his warships, to act as marines, and make themselves useful generally. Off Cape St. Vincent a Spanish fleet of about fourteen sail was sighted, and Rodney instantly signalled 'general chase', but could not close the enemy before nightfall, when the 'Moonlight Battle' commenced. During this engagement, Macleod's Highlanders hauled on the ropes and lined the bulwarks of their respective ships, firing their muskets whenever they got within range. Their numbers varied between 154 on the flagship, H.M.S. *Sandwich* and thirty on the frigates. It was an exciting experience of roaring broadsides, the deafening explosions of enemy ships blowing up, wild cheering and tempestuous seas, which, 'made it very difficult to take possession of those ships which had surrendered to His Majesty's arms'. It ended at two o'clock in the morning, when the enemy flagship *Monarco* struck to H.M.S. *Sandwich*, by which time over half the Spanish fleet had been taken or destroyed.

After the troops and supplies had been landed at the Rock, Rodney left with his fleet, and the siege continued for another thirteen months, with the garrison under continual bombardment by sea and land. The flank companies of Macleod's Highlanders (Grenadiers and Light Infantry) took part in the famous sortie of November 26, 1781, which destroyed the enemy land batteries; and the battalion was, of course, like the rest of the garrison, constantly in action along the perimeter defences. After a fleet had arrived under Lord Howe in October 1782, with reinforcements and supplies, the Spaniards realised that they had no hope of success and peace was signed in the following February, when the siege came to an end after lasting three years, seven months and twelve days. The 2nd battalion of Macleod's Highlanders returned home and was disbanded at Stirling in October, 1783. Its losses in the siege were 100 all-ranks killed and 121 wounded. It left to its descendants the device of the *Castle and Key, superscribed Gibraltar*, with the motto *Montis insignia Calpe*, borne on the colours of the Highland Light Infantry.

After the disbandment of the 2nd battalion, many of the officers and men, including George Mackenzie, volunteered to join the 1st battalion which, as related, had arrived at Madras in January, 1780. The position in Southern India was at that time precarious. The Hindu state of Mysore had been forcibly annexed by the Sultan Haidar Ali, a

The siege and relief of Gibraltar by J. S. Copley. Sir Gilbert Ellis issues his orders.

Mohammedan adventurer, who was determined to evict the British from the Carnatic. He was encouraged and assisted by the French whose fleet, under Admiral Suffren, cruised off the coast of Madras. The forces available to the British East India Company, consisting mostly of Hindu regiments, with a few British, were deplorably weak, and Macleod's Highlanders arrived only just in time to meet a major onslaught by Haidar Ali which carried him up to the walls of Madras.

In August, 1780, the British forces, which had been scattered throughout the Madras province, were ordered to concentrate at Conjeveram. This was successfully achieved, except for a small force under Colonel Baillie which was cut off. The flank companies of Macleod's marched to its assistance, but joined it only in time to fight to the last against overwhelming hordes of Mohammedans. The few wounded survivors of this affair, including Captain David Baird (afterwards General Sir David Baird, of whom more will be heard later) were thrown into the dungeons of Seringapatam, where they were kept for years, chained together in pairs. 'Heaven help the lad,' said his old mother, when she heard of Baird's fate, 'wha's chained to oor Davie!'

At the beginning of 1781, the ancient General Sir Eyre Coote took over command of the Madras army and, after marching around for hundreds of miles, attacked Haidar Ali at Porto Novo on July 1. The Sultan had about 100,000 men, whereas Coote could only muster about a tenth of that number, with Macleod's as his only King's—as opposed to Company's—regiment. Nevertheless, thanks to Macleod's Highlanders and his own tactical skill, he managed to get the better of the Sultan after a desperate and bloody battle. He had a dislike for the Highland bagpipe, but changed his mind after Porto Novo, during which he had seen Macleod's pipers playing the regiment into action. 'Well done, my brave fellow!' he shouted to one of them, 'you shall have silver pipes for this!' He was as good as his word, and in due course presented the regiment with a fine set of silver pipes, 'value 100 Pagodas', as a mark of appreciation. When presenting new colours to the Highland Light Infantry at the Delhi Durbar of 1911, King George V said, 'I cannot but remember, that if you had not been with Sir Eyre Coote at Porto Novo 130 years ago, I might not now be addressing you as Emperor of India'.

More long marches followed, and Macleod's were present at the relief of Vellore and the defeat of Haidar Ali at the battles of Sholinghur and Arnee, and the capture of Cuddalore, held by Haidar Ali's son, Tippu, and a French force, in 1783. Peace was signed in the following year, and the British captives, including David Baird, were returned. In January, 1786, new colours arrived for Macleod's Highlanders, and the number was changed from 73rd to 71st. As this number was held thereafter by the 1st battalion of the Highland Light Infantry, while the practice of calling a regiment by the name of its Colonel was discontinued, Macleod's Highlanders will now be referred to as the 71st.

In 1787, a treaty was concluded between France and Holland whereby the French arranged to garrison the Dutch possessions in India. This greatly encouraged the Sultan Tippu, who had succeeded on the death of his father, and greatly alarmed the East India Company, which asked the Home Government for reinforcements. Four new regiments were accordingly raised for service in India. One of these, the 74th Highland Regiment, later became the 2nd battalion of the Highland Light Infantry.

The first Colonel of the 74th was Major-General Sir Archibald Campbell of Inverneil who, like Lord Macleod, raised the regiment in his own clan country; in this case, Argyll. Just as the majority of the officers of the 71st were originally Mackenzies, so the majority of those of the 74th were Campbells—Campbells of Inverneil and Achalader, of Barbreck, Glensaddell and Strachur; of Achnacroish,

Achlian and Succoth, each of whom brought in his quota of recruits from his own part of Argyll, Kintyre and Knapdale. For a long time the 74th was in fact, known as 'the Argyle Regiment'. Like the 71st it also made up its numbers from the inexhaustible supplies of Glasgow, although that city was only a small town in those days,

Major Patrick Campbell of Barcalaig, 74th Highlanders, by J. S. Copley.

when there were plenty of salmon still left in the Clyde.

The 74th arrived in Madras in July and August, 1788. War with the Sultan of Mysore again broke out in the following year, when he invaded the State of Travancore, which Great Britain was bound by treaty to protect. All British-Indian troops in the three provinces of Madras, Bengal and Bombay were thereupon mobilized and the Governor-General in India, Lord Cornwallis, took personal command. He marched straight upon the Sultan's capital of Seringapatam, stopping on the way to capture the fortress of Bangalore, when the 'forlorn hope'[1] was provided by the 71st and the stormers by both 71st and 74th. Tippu then drew up his forces in front of Seringapatam, and was defeated in a battle in which both 71st and 74th distinguished themselves, but when he retired into the fortress, Cornwallis withdrew to Bangalore, having run out of supplies.

In 1792 Cornwallis again advanced on Seringapatam, having in the interim captured most of the Mysore fortresses. The 71st and 74th had each stormed some of these fortresses, many of which were formidable propositions. That of Pinagra, for instance, was perched on top of a high rock and surrounded by dense jungle. The 74th took it by storm against stout opposition, without the help of artillery, after climbing the rock and scaling the walls by makeshift ladders, losing six officers and sixty rank and file in killed and wounded.

Seringapatam was attacked in February, and the outlying works captured after desperate fighting during which the 71st and 74th engaged shoulder to shoulder. A work known as the Sultan's Redoubt was taken and held by Captain

---

[1] The forlorn hope was a small party which led the way into the breach and planted a flag on the ramparts to direct the stormers. Although commanded by an officer it was usually, by ancient custom, led by a sergeant who, if he survived, was rewarded with an Ensign's Commission.

Sibbald of the 71st who, when he was killed, was replaced by Major Skelly of the 74th. Tippu surrendered before the fortress itself was stormed, but he started fighting again in 1799, when a large British-Indian army under General Harris took the field against him. The 71st had left India in 1797, after taking part in some operations in Ceylon, but the 74th marched with Harris, in whose army a column was commanded by Colonel Arthur Wellesley, the future Duke of Wellington, who did not bother to hide his contempt for what he described as Harris' 'ponderous' methods of conducting a campaign.

Ponderous or not, Harris was entirely successful, and Seringapatam was taken by assault on May 4, 1799. The 74th were among the stormers, who were led by General Baird, only too rightly regarded by his mother as a most formidable character. He had volunteered for the honour of leading the stormers in order to get his own back on the Sultan, against whom he nourished a strong grievance bred in the Sultan's dungeons. Recognizing some old comrades in the ranks of the 74th: 'Ah! my lads!' he called to them, 'you and I are now going to pay off some old scores!'

The walls having been carried, the most desperate fighting followed inside the vast fortress. Tippu was wounded and unhorsed, when his servants tried to get him away in a palanquin. But the grenadiers of the 74th caught up with him, and one of them grabbed his jewelled sword-belt. The Sultan cut at him with his sword, and was shot dead and tumbled out among a heap of slain. Harris[1] accorded him a ceremonious martial funeral, during which the roar of the saluting guns was drowned by a heavy thunderstorm in which several persons were killed by lightning, making an awe-inspiring and fitting end to the career of a man known, in his life-time, as the 'Tiger of Mysore'.

[1] He was later created Lord Harris, and was the grandfather of the well-known England cricketer.

Peace was now restored to Mysore, where the ancient Hindu dynasty was reinstated. However, there was never any peace in the India of those days, disrupted as it was by the ambitions of warlike Princes, and the intrigues of competing European trading nations. Over in the Western Ghats was the country of the warrior Mahrattas, from which they sallied forth on horseback to plunder, kill and exort tribute. They were feared even as far as Calcutta, and had to be dealt with sooner or later. At their head was the Maharaja Scindia who, in previous conflicts with British forces, had been impressed—as all enemies of Great Britian were—by the British infantry. He had therefore raised a large corps of infantry trained on the British model and officered by Europeans—mostly French, although there were some Germans, and even British, among them.

After the fall of Seringapatam, the 74th spent some two years on operations conducted by Arthur Wellesley against the gangs of freebooters into which the Sultan's army had disintegrated, and they also took part in the Polygar campaign of 1801. At the beginning of 1803 however, the Mahrattas threatened the territories of the Nizam of Hyderabad, 'Faithful Ally of the British Empire', and the 74th joined a force under Wellesley—now a Major-General—which was sent to deal with them. The fortress of Ahmednaggar was stormed and captured in August, after which Wellesley marched against Scindia, who was on the other side of the Godavery river, which Wellesley's men crossed in goatskin coracles, constructed on the spot. Scindia retired through the pass of Adjunta and drew up in a strong position behind the river Kaitna, near the village of Assaye.

Wellesley arrived with his advanced guard at about one o'clock on the afternoon of September 23, 1803. He had about 6,000 men with him, of whom only the 72nd (Seaforth Highlanders), 74th Highlanders, and 19th Light Dragoons were British. The Mahratta host was 60,000 strong, horse, foot and guns, with European officers. Discerning a ford, Wellesley marched his army through it, with the Mahrattas making no move to stop him, and formed line of battle with the 74th on the right flank. He was then obliged to advance without delay, for the enemy were strong in artillery, which opened up and cut swathes through the British-Indian ranks. The native picquets, or skirmishers operating ahead of the 74th, lost direction and then ran back through the Highlanders, who were then charged in the flank by great numbers of Mahratta horse. In a desperate struggle, all of the eighteen officers of the 74th were cut down, with eleven of them dead, while of the 480 rank and file, 145 were killed and 250 wounded. The Quartermaster, James Grant, then ran forward from the baggage and took command; standing firm with the handful of survivors left on their feet. Their stand enabled Wellesley to advance his centre and left, take the Mahratta guns, and send their infantry flying with a cavalry charge. It was the first of all his innumerable victories in the field, and he never forgot the 74th for the part they played in it. In those days, the rope was commonly used as a deterrent to stop soldiers plundering, and Wellesley was as ruthless in its use as any. He would not however, permit a soldier of the 74th to suffer the ignoble death of hanging, whatever crime he might have committed.[1]

For their services on this day, the 74th were also given the unusual distinction of a third colour; the original being presented by the East India Company, and now laid up in Glasgow Cathedral. Known as the Assaye Colour, it has been carried ever since by the Highland Light Infantry. In addition, the regiment was granted the device of *The Elephant superscribed Assaye,* which was borne on the

---

[1] 'I think it very desirable to avoid punishing with death a soldier belonging to the 74th Regiment: and therefore I propose to offer to the man to commute his punishment to transportation for life to Botany Bay' (Wellesley's report to the Governor-General).

colours and also incorporated in the regimental badge.

In spite of their grievous losses, the 74th fought to the end of the Mahratta Campaign, taking part in the Battle of Argaum and the storming of Gwalighur. The regiment left India in 1805.

After five years in the United Kingdom, mostly spent in Ireland, and during which a second battalion was again raised, this time in Dumbarton, the 71st sailed in March, 1805, with an expedition sent under command of Sir David Baird to capture Cape Colony from the Dutch, in order to forestall its capture by the French. Baird succeeded in his

The Silhouette of an officer of the 74th Highlanders about 1830.

mission without difficulty; defeating the Dutch at the Battle of Blueberg by a charge of the Highland Brigade, composed of the 71st, 72nd and 93rd Highland Regiments. Unfortunately, the Commodore of the escort of warships, Sir Hume Popham, then decided to seek some prize-money and, hearing that there was a large sum of money in the Argentine Treasury at Buenos Ayres, determined upon securing it—for the Argentine, being a Spanish colony, and Great Britain being at war with Spain, was, according to Popham's way of thinking, open to having its treasury looted as a normal act of war.

For this expedition, Popham 'borrowed' the 71st Highlanders from Baird, who was Colonel of the regiment. He also obtained the services of Colonel Beresford to conduct the military operations. The 71st were landed at the mouth of the River Plate in June, 1806, and after a few engagements against cavalry and irregulars, captured Buenos Ayres and secured about 600,000 gold dollars. This treasure was sent home in a fast frigate, and gratefully received by the government, who sent reinforcements to Popham. Before they arrived however, Beresford had been forced to surrender in the face of national opposition. The 71st were given the Honours of War and placed on parole, from which they were released the following year under terms arranged by General Whitelock, who arrived with a strong expedition.

The 71st arrived in the United Kingdom in December, 1808, having not done too badly out of this strange affair. Their Colonel, David Baird, was the richer by £30,000, (although he had never left the Cape) and each private soldier got £18 6s. od.

Chapter 2

The Peninsular War

IN 1805, the year of Trafalgar, the 71st and 74th were both at sea during the anxious period when Napoleon was manœuvring his fleets in an attempt to gain control of the Channel and mount an invasion of England. The 71st were outward-bound for the Cape and the 74th homeward-bound for the Clyde. After arriving home, the 74th were quartered in Dumbarton Castle. It is distressing to relate that their total strength in all-ranks amounted only to 165, which means that the bones of nearly a thousand officers and men lay scattered over Southern India, or at the bottom of the ocean. Those of the gallant Quartermaster, James Grant, who had led the remains of the regiment out of action at Assaye, were among the latter, for he had died during the voyage home. He had been one of the first to enlist in the 74th Highlanders, and before his death had been heard to remark that, during seventeen years service in the regiment he had known three completely different sets of officers; so grievous were the casualties suffered in an unending series of hard-fought campaigns, and so heavy the toll exacted from suffering and disease.

However, when a man such as Napoleon was at large on the Continent, there was nothing gained from sorrowing over fallen comrades. Great Britain was fighting for her very existence, and the ranks had to be filled. The 74th left Dumbarton Castle and marched all over the Highlands to recruit. One of their recruits was James Ross, the only survivor out of four brothers of whom the other three were all killed in the Peninsular War. In 1882 he was still alive at the age of 95; living in the house which he and his brothers had purchased for their parents out of their enlistment bounties. 'The 74th!' he related to an officer of the regiment who visited him, 'they were marching from Fort George by Aberdeen and Forfar to the West. I went out the length of Finavon to meet them. Braw they looked, in feathered bonnets and the kilt. The first I met was an officer riding, and I speired at him gin he would list me? He said I was ower young and maun bide a wee. The next year I listed wi' a Lieutenant MacLean. Oh aye, it was a commissioned officer 'listed me! There were plenty going about at the time; the country was fair fu' o' bagpipes and drums and fifes, wi' the recruiters; and big bounties we got —twal and whiles twenty guineas'.

However, able-bodied men who were not already serving were none too easy to find in Scotland at that time. After two years of beating their drums and sounding their bagpipes, the 74th had only collected 700, and so adopted the customary expedient of crossing to Ireland to make up their establishment—for an Irishman was more-or-less indifferent as to what uniform he wore, so long as there was a chance of getting into a fight. The 71st were already in that country for the same reason but, just as the 74th arrived, in 1808, they sailed from Cork with Sir Arthur Wellesley, bound for Portugal.

The whole of the Peninsula was at this time in the grip of Napoleon, but the Spaniards had risen in revolt, and when the Portuguese followed their example the British government dispatched a force under Wellesley with orders to clear the French out of Portugal. Wellesley landed near Lisbon and defeated Marshal Junot at Roleia, where only the light company of the 71st was engaged. The rest of the regiment was 'manœuvring all day to turn their flank; so that our fatigue was excessive, though our loss was but small'. Wellesley then took up a defensive position at Vimiera to cover the disembarkation of reinforcements, and here Junot attacked him on August 21. During the desperate engagement which followed, the 71st were on the left flank. Five French guns and a howitzer were captured with their horses by the grenadier company, and General Brennier, who was trying to get round Wellesley's left, was captured by Corporal Mackay of the 71st, who was rewarded by an Ensign's commission. Piper George Clark also distinguished himself at Vimiera. He was badly wounded in the groin while playing his company forward, but remarking 'Deil ha' my saul, if ye shall want music', continued his tune while stretched bleeding on the ground. He was presented with a set of silver-mounted bagpipes by the Highland Society of London, in recognition of his conduct.

The victory of Vimiera was followed by the Convention of Cintra, signed by the opposing commanders, under which the French were evacuated from Portugal in British

At the battle of Vimiera the 71st took Gen. Brennier prisoner.

ships and returned to France. In spite of his successes, Wellesley fell into disgrace for his part in these arrangements, and was relieved by Sir John Moore.

Marching in two columns, Moore crossed into Spain in November, 1808, but found the Spaniards unco-operative and eventually got into difficulties, with Marshal Soult on one side of him and Napoleon himself on the other. Thus

Army Museums Ogilby Trust

George Clark piper of the 71st Highlanders with pipes presented to him after the Battle of Vimiera, 1808.

began the dreadful retreat across the mountains to Corunna, in the depth of winter and harassed by Soult's cavalry. Like most of the army, the 71st were starving and in rags, marching either in bare feet or with them bound up in pieces of blanket. Nevertheless, they held together somehow, beating off all French attacks, and Moore was able to form line of battle on arriving at Corunna in January. There was no sign of his transports, and he was therefore obliged to turn and fight Soult, who advanced against him on January 15, 1809. The 71st were sent out to cover the concentration, and fell back skirmishing with the French, afterwards taking post on the left wing. Soult attacked on the right, so that the regiment was not at first engaged, but it was later transferred to the other flank; passing on its way the mortally wounded Sir John Moore being carried from the field. He had fallen at the moment of victory, and the army was able to embark without interference from the enemy.

Shortly after their return from Corunna, the 71st became a Light Infantry regiment; joining the *corps d'elite* which had in fact been started by Sir John Moore. It was regarded as a high honour to have been so selected, but the regiment was a good deal worried about the possible effect on its Highland status and traditions. The authorities were at first unsympathetic, but at length agreed to the regiment being re-named the Highland Light Infantry, and retaining its pipers thus keeping, in the words of its Colonel, 'the honourable characteristics . . . which must preserve to future times the precious remains of the old corps, and of which I feel confident His Majesty will never have reason to deprive the 71st Regiment'.

In spite of their arduous experiences in Spain, the 71st were not allowed to remain idle long. At the end of April, 1809, they paraded at Gosport, over a thousand strong, having completed their training as light infantry. 'As beautiful a regiment as ever I saw', was how one of the

3

soldiers proudly described it. The regiment embarked in one of a fleet of thirty-five sail of the line and twenty-three frigates, with nearly 200 other vessels, assembled for the capture of the island of Walcheren and the destruction of the French fleet lying in the Scheldt. 'His Majesty could have wished,' wrote old King George III, 'that the information upon which the practicability of the expedition has been finally decided had not been so imperfect.' His forebodings were unfortunately disregarded, and in due course the 71st led the way ashore and were soon in action against enemy skirmishers. Having disposed of these, they moved along the sea wall against the fortified town of Veere, during the capture of which they lost thirty-five men in killed and wounded. On August 3, the siege of Flushing was opened, and during the night of the fourteenth the 71st crept along the dyke and climbed the ramparts on the eastern side. They were led by their Colonel, Denis Pack, who got within arm's length of an enemy sentry without being noticed, and struck off the unfortunate fellow's head with one blow of his sword.

Flushing capitulated on the following day, so that the expedition up to that point had not been unsuccessful. The enemy however, had opened the dykes, so that the whole country was under water and a typhoid epidemic broke out which finally led to the evacuation of the island without any useful purpose having been achieved. The 71st returned home in December in a very sickly condition, having lost twenty-one in action and sixty-nine from 'Walcheren Fever'. According to one soldier, the latter figures would have been far greater had it not been for a medicine composed of brandy and gunpowder; the preparation of which had been taught to the 71st by the sailors of H.M.S. *Belleisle* during the passage to Walcheren.

Following Soult's repulse at Corunna, Napoleon had reorganized his forces in Spain and formed an 'Army of Portugal', commanded by Marshal Massena, who had orders to re-occupy Portugal and drive the British into the sea. The British army in Portugal, was once again under the command of Wellesley, who had come back into favour and was now Lord Wellington. Being far too weak in numbers to take any offensive action, he had taken up a position along the Spanish frontier, and commenced the construction of the Lines of Torres Vedras for the ultimate defence of Lisbon should, as he anticipated, he be obliged to retire. On March 16, 1810, he was advised of the arrival of the 74th Highlanders, to whom he owed a great deal. 'My fighting regiment', he called them; and he at once rode out from his headquarters at Viseu to greet them on the line of march.

The 74th, having obtained their quota of Irishmen, had sailed from the Cove of Cork in January, and were now in fine fettle and well able to return Wellington's searching stare without flinching. He could scarcely have avoided thinking of the day, nearly seven years before, when at Assaye after ordering a general advance, he had galloped across to the 74th on his right, to find only forty men where there should have been 500, and the commanding-officer, Samuel Swinton, lying in his blood with his back propped against the body of his slain charger.

'Get the 74th forward, Swinton! Where the devil are the rest of 'em?' 'They are all down Sir.'

Many years after he had fought his last campaign, when so many other stirring and tragic recollections must have filled his mind, the Duke of Wellington would still relate this incident, which had so affected him at the time that he had spent the night after the battle sleepless, crouched with his head in his hands.

Massena advanced on September 15, 1810. Wellington, slowly retiring before him, lured his opponent towards 'a most excellent position', along a ridge at Busaco, where he trounced him severely on September 27. This was the first action fought by the 74th in the Peninsular War, and they were still raw and inexperienced. They had been posted to the 3rd, or 'Fighting Division', led by that singular character Picton, an uncouth though capable warrior, 'full of strange oaths', and never really happy out of musket shot of the French. As a rule, Wellington formed his line under the crest of a hill, both for concealment and cover from artillery fire, but some troops of course, had to watch the forward slope, and at Busaco the 74th had the misfortune to be lined up in the open, having to endure the preliminary bombardment without even being allowed to lie down. After some time of being knocked about by cannon-balls, they became a bit restive, and their unprintable comments were heard by their Colonel, le Poer Trench, above the roar of the guns. He rode down the line, sternly bidding them to keep silence, and to 'remember Assaye'. This quietened them, and when the French arrived they were ready for them. Two companies were ordered forward against the enemy skirmishers, and advanced with a will. 'The pleasure I experienced,' wrote one of the officers, 'in advancing on the enemy instead of remaining exposed and inactive as we were cannot be expressed.' The same pleasure was shared by all the soldiers, who chased the enemy down to the bottom of the slope. Here they got into trouble with masses of Frenchmen, and came up again almost as quickly as they had gone down, only to run into Picton himself. 'Halt there!' he roared, 'Halt, I say! Rally on me, damn your eyes!' So they faced about once more and, with the remainder of the regiment held off all-comers until the advance was ordered, and the French routed at the bayonet-point.

His victory at Busaco enabled Wellington to withdraw behind his fortified Lines of Torres Vedras. Before he reached them, his army was joined by the 71st, who had sailed from the Cove on the same day that Massena crossed the frontier into Portugal. The regiment was first in action at Sobral, a village held as a covering position, where the 71st picquets were attacked on October 12. One of the picquets was overrun, and obliged to make a precipitous retreat over a high wall, leaving John Rae, the oldest soldier of the regiment and 'a man of gloomy disposition, in short, a Methodist', behind. His advanced years made it impossible for Rae to skip over the wall like the others, so he stood his ground and, having shot one Frenchman and bayoneted two others, clambered over with the help of his comrades who later, with the approval of the Brigadier and Colonel, both of whom had seen the incident, presented Rae with an inscribed medal made out of a silver dollar. Both regular battalions of the future Highland Light Infantry were now in the field, so that with but very few exceptions, all major engagements in the Peninsular War were commemorated on its colours.

The Lines of Torres Vedras proving impregnable, and the whole countryside having been laid waste by its inhabitants under Wellington's orders, Massena was obliged to retreat into Spain in the spring of 1811. He was closely followed by Wellington, and both the 71st and 74th were constantly in action against the French rear-guards, commanded by Marshal Ney. The hardship and suffering endured by both sides during this period were such as to strain the imagination, and it is difficult to say which was the worse off. The first major action was fought out on May 3, 1811, when Massena, hearing that Wellington was absent on reconnaisance, attacked the British right at Fuentes d'Onor. Wellington fortunately returned just after this key position had been overrun, and ordered the 71st, supported by the 79th and 24th Regiments, to re-capture it. On getting his orders Cadogan, the Colonel of the 71st, called to his men and, pointing to the village, shouted 'My lads! you have had nothing to eat for two days. There's biscuits and rum in that village. Come and get it!'

As the exhausted 71st, who had covered sixty miles on empty stomachs in the previous three days, doubled forward into action, one soldier had his knapsack neatly removed from his shoulders by 'an obliging cannon-ball'. Fuentes d'Onor was packed with Frenchmen: 'At 'em, 71st!' shouted the Colonel, 'charge 'em down the Gallowgate!' This somewhat obscure reference to a street in Glasgow, with an ancient barracks at the end of it, seems to have been fully understood by the soldiers, who closed with the enemy and, after a desperate struggle, threw them out of the village. They counter-attacked with four fresh battalions, and the battle raged back and forth till nightfall, by which time the streets had become so blocked with corpses that it was difficult to move. An exchange of wounded was made under a flag of truce, and the French withdrew, leaving the 71st to enjoy their first meal for nearly three days—not rum and biscuits, but four ounces of bread apiece, which had been 'collected out of the haversacks of the Foot Guards'.

In the later stages of the struggle for the village the 74th who, with Picton's Division, had been keeping the right flank, were sent in to reinforce the 71st and the others in Fuentes d'Onor, and took part in the final charge which settled the issue and decided the day. Wellington felt more relief than elation at his victory. 'If Boney had been here,' he remarked, 'we'd have been damnably licked.'

Shortly after this affair General Beresford, who was besieging Badajoz, was attacked by Soult, and just managed to get the best of it at Albuera. Wellington marched to his support with Picton's and the 7th Divisions, and reopened the siege, but when Soult returned he declined battle and moved north to besiege Ciudad Rodrigo. Here he was attacked by Marshal Marmont, who had relieved Massena in command of the 'Army of Portugal'. During a fighting withdrawal across the Coa, the 74th became detached from the remainder of the 3rd Division and were given up for lost, except by Picton, who said that 'he would have expected to hear more firing before the 74th could be captured'. He was quite right, for the regiment turned up in due course, having marched and fought itself to a standstill. Over 100, in fact, could no longer move, and had to be carried over the river.

At this time, Wellington sent his compliments to the 71st for their conduct at Fuentes d'Onor, and asked for the name of a non-commissioned officer for promotion in the field. The name of Quartermaster-Sergeant Gavin was submitted, and shortly afterwards he was commissioned as

Sir George Napier as a Lieut.-Colonel of 71st Highland Light Infantry. By Sigurac painted in 1814. He is wearing Ciudad Rodrigo Gold Medal—where he lost an arm in 1812.

Ensign in the regiment. Battle casualties, which included 127 fallen at Fuentes d'Onor, had reduced the 71st to under 200 effectives, so that they had been relieved, and were temporarily out of action.

The campaign of 1812 opened early with the capture of the strong fortress of Ciudad Rodrigo during the night of January 14. The stormers consisted of 500 men of the 74th under Major Manners, who attacked through the 'Great Breach', and made it good enabling the Light Division to enter the 'Small Breach' and force the surrender of the garrison after some hard fighting.

Badajoz, to which Wellington now turned his attention, was a far more difficult proposition. Any lengthy siege was out of the question, for it would be certain to be interrupted by Soult and Marmont so that, in order to get it done quickly he was obliged to use almost his entire force which, after leaving a garrison at Ciudad Rodrigo and sending off Sir Rowland Hill to keep an eye on Soult, amounted to about 20,000 men.

The 71st, who had received a draft of 350 recruits, had been with Hill for some time, and had accompanied him on a raid into Estramadura, on which they had distinguished themselves at Arroyo Molinos. While the siege of Badajoz was in progress, Hill advanced on Almaraz, with the object of destroying the bridge of boats laid across the Tagus, and thus preventing a junction between Soult and Marmont. This exploit was successfully carried out on May 19, with the 71st again proving their worth in close action. More than once, as they marched and countermarched on these operations they came within sound of Wellington's guns at Badajoz, and on each occasion Colonel Cadogan got a supply of rum from somewhere, and made all ranks drink upstanding to, 'the valour of the stormers and the success of British arms'.

The siege of Badajoz had opened in the middle of March, with assaults on the outlying forts Picherina and San Roque.

The former was stormed by Picton's Division during the night of the twenty-fifth, and taken after heavy fighting in which the 74th lost two officers and about fifty men. The siege train of thirty-eight guns then opened against the curtain wall of the main fortress, and for ten days poured in a ceaseless hail of shot. The breach in the masonry then being considered 'practicable' the assault was ordered for the night of April 5 but, as Wellington seldom went into battle without attempting to hoodwink the enemy in some way, he ordered Picton to make a feint attack against the castle, in order to divert the attention of the garrison from the breach.

The medieval castle, with its high, turreted wall and lofty tower, stood at the north-east angle of the fortress on the top of a grassy slope so steep as to be precipitous in many places. A wall twenty feet high stood between it and the flooded tributary Roillas. It was unscathed by gun-fire, and the possibility of its capture scarcely entered Wellington's mind. Picton however, never had any use for feint attacks, but always drove home, no matter what the odds were against him. 'Some persons are of the opinion that the attack upon the castle will not succeed,' he told his officers, 'but I will forfeit my life, if it does not.' Marching off in the pitch darkness, he led his division across the Roillas, by way of a narrow dam, two feet under water and as slippery as ice. A certain amount of noise, and the showing of a light alerted the garrison, who opened a heavy fire on the dam, causing heavy casualties with Picton himself among them, badly wounded in the leg. Colonel Kemp took over from him and pressed on: The curtain wall being scaled and the ladders erected against the keep, up went the soldiers led by their officers, many of whom were mere boys in their teens; but they were bayoneted at the top, the ladders overturned, and everyone on them flung down the slope into the water.

At this junction Picton arrived, hobbling with his leg in

splints, and roaring like a bull. Finding a part of the wall which had not been tried, he sent the 5th Fusiliers up the ladders and took the French by surprise. The 74th went up another part of the wall, with Piper MacLauchlan one of the first. Once on the ramparts he started *The Campbells are Coming;* the ancient march of the clan, which was still the battle-tune of the 74th—'The Argyle Regiment'. A bullet through the bag of his pipes failed to stop his music for long. Seated nonchalantly on a gun-carriage, and ignoring the turmoil going on around him, he mended the hole and the inspiring air once again sounded above the walls of Badajoz.

After a desperate resistance, the survivors of the garrison fled into the town, pursued by Lieutenant Alexander Grant of the 74th, at the head of a few of his men. They were driven back through the gate and Grant, the last man in, was mortally wounded.

The unexpected seizure of the castle by the Fighting Division sealed the fate of Badajoz. The main assaults had been repelled at the breaches after two hours of desperate fighting by the 4th and Light Divisions, and Wellington's iron nerve had broken for a moment as he realized that all the effort and sacrifice had been in vain. He was just about to give orders for a retirement, when a galloper arrived. 'General Picton sends compliments, m'lord, and begs to say the 3rd Division is in full possession of the castle.' A renewed attack succeeded at the San Vicente bastion and the French, with the heart gone out of them, retired within Fort Christobal, where they surrendered on the following morning.

The storming of Badajoz cost Wellington some 5,000 killed and wounded, including five general officers. The losses suffered by the 74th amounted to sixteen officers, including the commanding-officer, and 120 rank and file. But the prize was well worth this heavy cost, for with the fortresses of Elvas, Almeida, Ciudad Rodrigo and Badajoz in British hands, Portugal was safe from invasion, and the initiative had passed to Wellington; which meant that the expulsion of the French from Spain by this great soldier was only a matter of time.

At the beginning of June, 1812, Wellington marched against Marmont, whose 'Army of Portugal', was concentrated round Salamanca. The French Marshals had now begun to treat Wellington with considerable respect, realizing that he knew rather more about the profession of arms than they did themselves. Marmont accordingly declined battle and started manœuvring, with the object of heading Wellington away from his lines of communication. Both armies, after marching and counter-marching, sometimes within musket-shot of each other, eventually got back to Salamanca where, on July 22, Wellington saw that his opponent was vulnerable and attacked; first sending in the 3rd Division. As Picton had gone home to recover from his wound, the Fighting Division was under the command of Sir Edward Pakenham, Wellington's brother-in-law. 'Ned!' shouted Wellington, galloping up, 'move on with the 3rd Division, take the heights to your front, and drive everything before you!'

The advance of the 3rd Division thus started the Battle of Salamanca, at which '40,000 men were beaten in forty minutes', as a French officer remarked afterwards. The 74th, who were in the thick of it, came off lightly with losses of two officers and forty-seven rank and file. Their admirable alignment, when closing with the enemy, attracted the attention of Pakenham, who took the trouble to canter over to them and cry 'beautifully done, 74th! *beautifully done!*' Marmont was severely wounded in the action, and the French completely routed, with losses of nearly 15,000 men and twelve guns. Wellington marched as far as Valladolid in pursuit, capturing many prisoners and much booty, and then turned on Madrid, where Napoleon's brother Joseph had been acting-monarch, since the deposition of the King of Spain. Joseph hastily evacuated the capital, which Wellington entered on August 12 to a rousing welcome from the citizens which was shared by the 74th, who afterwards spent two pleasant months in the city. The regiment thus did not accompany Wellington when he marched against Burgos in September.

At Burgos, Wellington encountered the combined armies of Soult and Joseph, and was obliged to retreat to Ciudad Rodrigo, being joined on the way by Sir Rowland Hill's Division in which the 71st marched, and the 3rd Division with the 74th.

The 71st and 74th were both present and distinguished themselves at the brilliant and decisive victory of Vittoria, fought on June 21, 1813. Napoleon had been obliged to withdraw large numbers of his troops from Spain, to make up for his devastating losses in his abortive Russion campaign, so that, for the first time, Wellington was able to take the field at a strength more or less equal to the enemy, taking into consideration the Portuguese army (led by Sir Denis Pack, formerly commanding-officer of the 71st) and the Spanish forces, which were now under his command. For the first time also, he was able to take full advantage of the British command of the sea, and supply his forces through the Biscayan ports as he advanced, while constantly threatening the French supply routes by thrusting forward his left wing.

After turning the enemy flank on the Douro, and again on the Ebro, he brought them to bay before Vittoria where King Joseph, against the advice of his chief-of-staff, Marshal Jourdain, felt obliged to give battle rather than submit to being hustled out of Spain without a fight. The engagement opened with an attack by Sir Rowland Hill against the French left, which was strongly posted on the Heights of Puebla. These heights were quickly secured by a Spanish brigade, but immediately recaptured by an enemy counter-attack. The 71st were then sent in, and after

Army Museums Ogilby Trust

The heroic death of Lt. Col. Hon. Henry Cadogan, 71st Highland Light Infantry, at the Battle of Vittoria, 1813.

a most desperate struggle at close quarters drove the French across a ravine. Unfortunately Colonel Cadogan was mortally wounded, and after a brave attempt to keep control while lying at the point of death on a small hillock, was obliged to hand over to Major Cother, who led the regiment across the ravine into dense masses of Frenchmen. The 71st were only saved from complete annihilation by the timely arrival of the 50th regiment and the 92nd High-landers. Repeated French counter-attacks were beaten off, and the heights eventually secured, but at a cost to the 71st of their Colonel, fourteen other officers, and 301 rank and file killed and wounded.

The 74th, in Brisbane's brigade, had meanwhile crossed the Bayas river and advanced on Arinez. They were exchanging shots with the French at close range when Wellington galloped up to Picton, whom he found 'in a blue coat and round hat swearing with the strength of fifty devils'. Leaving him to swear in peace, Wellington led off Brisbane's brigade and drove the French from Arinez, where the 74th captured three guns with their teams. The brigade should then have re-formed, but the 88th dashed in among the French and the 74th followed. The adjutant, Major White, was sent to call them back and told John MacLauchlan, the piper, to sound the gathering. 'Where-upon,' wrote Major White, 'all those that were not shot gathered round me. I told MacLauchlan that I would not fail to mention his gallant and useful conduct. But at the same time as I turned my horse to conduct the men towards our Regiment, a musket ball entered the point of my left shoulder to near my backbone, which stopped my career in the field.'

The general advance was then ordered and the 74th, now down to about 300 all-ranks, moved forward in line across very broken ground, so that the colours, in the centre, had to be constantly exposed and waved, to enable the regiment to keep its formation and direction. The enemy fire was naturally directed against the colours and John MacLauchlan, who was playing behind them, was struck by a cannon-ball which smashed his legs into pulp. Nevertheless, he asked those near by to hand him back his pipes, and went on playing until he died. The regiment was greatly upset by his death, which had a curious sequel. The dead and wounded on the Peninsular battlefields were nearly always stripped by the local peasants, but when those at Vittoria were being picked up afterwards, it was found that John MacLauchlan's body had alone been respected, and that his silver-mounted pipes, sword and dirk were still with it.

In his brigade orders after the battle, General Brisbane wrote that 'He is at a loss to express his admiration of the conduct of the Honourable Colonel le Poer Trench and the 74th Regiment, which he considers contributed much to the success of the day'.

Chapter
3
Waterloo, Canada, The Kaffir War

AFTER Vittoria the French withdrew to the Pyrenees, and Napoleon, realizing that the south of France was now in danger, sent Soult to take over command. Soult developed an attack through the Pyrenees towards the British right at Pamplona. In its initial stages his advance brought in the 71st who, in Cameron's brigade of Sir Rowland Hill's corps, was at the Pass of Baztan, which was attacked on the morning of July 25 by General d'Erlon with three French divisions. The pass was held by two weak British brigades, which for ten hours withstood an attack by five times their number of French. The 71st ran out of ammunition but, with no thought of withdrawal, stood fast with their bayonets, and rolled boulders down the hillside on the enemy as opportunity offered. General Stewart, who was in command, had reached the stage of riding round calling out, 'let us stand to the last', when the arrival of a fresh British brigade turned the scale; the French were driven back in disorder and the pass held.

Soult was unaware of this setback when he engaged Wellington at Sorauren. A premature withdrawal of the 3rd Division by Picton from Huarte, to his front, made things awkward for the Duke but nevertheless, he got the better of Soult on the actual battlefield and drove him back. The 74th were engaged both at Huarte and Sorauren but, owing to Picton unaccountably losing his nerve, got no opportunity for distinguishing themselves. During the subsequent advance however, they attacked the French rearguard and accounted for some 1,500 of the enemy, at a cost to themselves of six officers, including Colonel le Poer Trench, and forty-three rank and file.

Taking Soult by surprise, Wellington forced the passage of the Bidassoa on October 7, and established his forward troops on French soil. The 71st and 74th were both on outpost duty at this time, watching the mountain passes under conditions of great hardship, for the snow was knee-deep, the cold excrutiating, their only cover was the bivouac shelter constructed out of one or two worn blankets, and food was very short indeed. Both regiments had lost well over half their numbers in battle-casualties during the preceding two months; the strength of the 71st having fallen from 984 rank and file to 395, with an even heavier drop in the roll of officers. The 71st was the only light infantry regiment in its division, and tended therefore, to get a good deal more than its fair share of hard fighting, for the general was always shouting 'let the 71st go forward!' whenever the enemy appeared in front. There were no complaints, however, and the fact that, after all these years the French were at last on the run, provided a very powerful stimulus to morale.

On October 31, the fortress of Pampluna surrendered to Wellington, which secured his position in Spain, and on November 10, he attacked Soult along the Nivelle. Sir Rowland Hill's Corps turned the French position at Ainhoa, without having to call up his reserve brigade, so that for once in a way the 71st did not go into action. The 74th however, attacked the French right at Sarre, where the fighting was of the most bitter description, and afterwards charged and carried the enemy bridgehead at Amotz. They lost six officers and sixty-three rank and file in this fighting, which they could ill-afford out of their reduced strength.

Soult then retired beyond the Nive, where he again failed to hold Wellington, who crossed on December 9. About three weeks previously, the 71st had been sent forward to capture the village of Cambo, on the left bank of this

4

river, and had done so at the cost of forty-eight casualties. They were still holding the village, and guarding the broken bridge over the Nive, when Wellington came up to reconnoitre on the day before the battle. The river was forded at dawn on the following day, with the 71st in the lead, coming under heavy fire while up to their necks in water. The day ended with Hill's corps across the river, cut off from the main army, and offering an excellent opportunity for Soult which he endeavoured to exploit by attacking Hill on December 13. The Battle of St. Pierre followed, during which all Hill could do was to act on the defensive, without hope of succour from Wellington. The fighting raged all day, with the French launching repeated attacks, all of which were beaten off, but at a cost to the 71st of twelve officers and 127 rank and file in killed and wounded. The regiment had received two drafts of officers and men before leaving Spain, but nevertheless, its strength when it came out of action at St. Pierre could not have been much above 200.

After the Battle of St. Pierre, Hill's corps was sent forward to the Adour to threaten the French left, and a pause ensued which lasted until February 14, 1814, when Wellington invested Bayonne on his left, and commenced the operations known as 'the passage of the Gaves', on his right. The 71st and 74th were both engaged in the latter, and had some hard fighting preparatory to the Battle of Orthez, which took place on February 27. The 74th, who advanced with the 3rd Division against the enemy's centre, had more to do on this day than the 71st who, with Hill's corps, were unable to cross the Adour until the field was won and the French in retreat. The 71st therefore came off lightly with a few men wounded, while the 74th lost five officers and thirty-seven rank and file. The conduct of the 74th was recognized after the battle in the usual manner, by the regiment being invited to submit the name of a warrant-officer for promotion in the field. The name of

John Macpherson, the R.S.M., was forwarded, and he was promoted in due course to the rank of Ensign.

Soult having withdrawn to Toulouse, Wellington's final advance then started in a deluge of rain, in which a number of minor, though bloody engagements took place against the French rearguards. The hardest fought of these affairs took place near Tarbes on March 19, when both the 71st and 74th were in action and 'lost some men'.

The Battle of Toulouse was fought on April 10, 1814. Neither Soult nor Wellingt on unfortunately were aware that Napoleon had abdicated, and that the war was at an end, so that the lives of thousands of men were sacrificed to no purpose. As Hill's corps was committed only to a holding attack against the fortified suburb of St. Cyprien, the 71st were lightly engaged, and lost but three men killed, but the 74th were tragically unlucky. Picton, like Hill, had also been ordered to make a holding attack which was not intended to be pressed home, but Picton, as already mentioned in the account of Badajoz, was not the man for holding attacks. Once he smelt blood, there was no holding him. The 3rd Division went into action along the north side of the Languedoc canal, and carried all before it until the 74th were held up at the bridge at Jumeaux, which was defended by a palisade too high to be scaled without ladders, and approached across open ground without cover of any kind. A close reconnaisance was made at great risk by Major Alves, the adjutant, who reported that the palisades were impassable without artillery. He was sent to make his report to Picton, only to be sternly ordered, 'Go back, Sir, and tell them to move on.' Alves rode back with this message, 'with a heavy heart', and the 74th, 350 strong, advanced accordingly through a murderous enfilade fire from both flanks. Reaching the palisades, several desperately gallant but fruitless efforts were made to scale them without ladders, after which the regiment retired back the way it had come, leaving behind nine officers and 132 rank and file killed and wounded. One of them was Captain Donald MacQueen, veteran of nine general engagements with a scar to show for each of them. Now he lay shot through both lungs, and in sore straits, but was picked up by his foster-brother, John Gillanders, a private in the regiment, who had joined with MacQueen when he received his commission. Gillanders carried him out of range and tried to find a bed for him in one of the houses near-by, but they were all packed with wounded men, and all his tears and entreaties were in vain. Eventually a bed was given up by Sir Thomas Brisbane, the Brigadier, who, though badly wounded himself, remarked that MacQueen 'needs the bed more than I do'. MacQueen recovered, and lived until 1830, ending his career as a Major, and a Military Knight of Windsor. It is to be hoped that the story of Gillanders had an equally happy ending, but there is unfortunately no record of the fate of this devoted but humble individual.

During the night the French withdrew from Toulouse, which Wellington entered on the following day. Shortly afterwards officers arrived from Paris with the news of the Emperor's abdication, and the termination of hostilities. What was left of the 74th took part in the triumphal entry into Toulouse, and the regiment remained billeted in the city until it returned home. Both the 71st and 74th were then stationed in Ireland.

Although the war with Imperial France was over, that against the United States continued, and the majority of British infantry regiments were sent off to America soon after arriving home. The 71st was among them, but the vessel in which they embarked was delayed at Cork by foul winds for nearly two months, during which Napoleon escaped from Elba, and the destination was changed to Belgium.

Landing at Ostend, the 71st marched to Leuze, about 1,000 strong, and joined the Light Brigade, commanded by Major-General Sir Frederick Adam. It arrived on the field of Waterloo late in the evening of June 17, after marching for thirty-six hours without food, and with no halt longer than half-an-hour; for the matter was urgent, to say the least of it. Wellington had been, as he put it, 'humbugged, by God!' by Napoleon's rapid and skilful manœuvres, and his army had to exert itself in order to bar the way to Brussels.

A drenching rain fell steadily all night, so that the misery of the exhausted soldiers of the 71st, over half of whom were raw recruits, may be imagined. However, it was fine for the actual battle, and as Napoleon decided to wait until the ground dried a little before he attacked, Wellington's men had time to cook themselves a meal. Adam's Light Brigade was stationed on the right of the allied line, opposite the farm of Hougoumont, which was held as an advanced post by the light companies of the Guards.

The French advance was heralded by a furious cannonade, which went on for a considerable time. It was directed chiefly against the allied right, and the 71st in particular had a hard time of it, drawn up in close column in the open. When they advanced at last, they left some seventy killed and wounded on the ground behind them.

During the day, the 71st repulsed no less than seven enemy cavalry charges, each time forming square which, on one occasion sheltered the Duke of Wellington himself. Unlike Napoleon, who stayed at his headquarters, Wellington was constantly riding about, attended by an orderly, and it was only the speed of his famous charger, Copenhagen, which saved him from the French cavalry which, unable to break the British squares, hung round Wellington's position 'as if they had been our own'.

Just before 8 o'clock in the evening, Napoleon sent forward his last reserve of 3,500 of the Imperial Guard. They were met by the musket volleys of the British Guards, and while reeling under the shock, the 52nd Light Infantry, on the left of the 71st, charged them in the flank. The 71st immediately wheeled left and also charged, coming up again on the right of the 52nd. Thrown into disorder, the Imperial Guard staggered back down the slope, and at this moment Wellington gave the order, 'the field is won, let the whole line advance'. The 71st moved forward accordingly, and appear from their position to have been the foremost British troops at this stage. On reaching the Charleroi road, they found the Imperial Guard attempting to rally, but a volley from the regiment got them on the move again, and the 71st then charged and captured their reserve battery of artillery. One of the guns, which were still loaded, was turned round and fired at the retreating French; and this is said to have been the last shot fired at Waterloo.

'I thought,' wrote Ensign Impett to his mother, 'that it was as well riding as walking; so I cut a famous horse out of a battery, and mounted him.' This seemed to his brother officers, and the rank and file of the 71st, to be a good idea

71st Highlanders, Waterloo, June 18, 1815. The 71st fire the last shot of the day.

and, as there was no lack of stray horses on the tragic field of Waterloo, what was left of the regiment was soon all mounted. It seems in fact, that the 71st rode all the way to Paris unquestioned, in the general confusion, by any officer in authority.

After serving for three years with the army of occupation, the 71st moved to Ireland, and then to Canada in 1824. A brief spell in Scotland was then followed by a second tour in Canada, commencing in 1838, when the regiment became involved in a rebellion by the French Canadians with the support of the Americans. This trouble was quickly suppressed, but the 71st had one brush with the rebels at Beauharnois, whither the regiment was marching, accompanied by the Glengarry Regiment of Canadian Militia and some Red Indians. The Glengarries were all Highland immigrants and were dressed in worn-out plaids, brogues and shabby bonnets. The 71st thought them 'a rum-looking set of raggamuffins'; forgetting that their own get-up was a bit peculiar too.

Presentation of Colours to the 71st, May 19, 1837 by Major Gen. Sir Edward Blakeney, K.C.B.

It appears that the Duke of Wellington, who was not normally interested in what soldiers wore, had been, while in Paris after Waterloo, struck by the shabby appearance of the British regiments in contrast to the magnificence of the Continental armies. The result was a new issue of uniform, designed by the Prince Regent, and consisting of a high bell-topped shako; a tight-fitted scarlet jacket with tails; a mass of pipe-clay and gold lace, and, in the case of the 71st, 'trowsers', of Mackenzie tartan. The 74th, and most of the other Highland regiments, were similarly clad but, of course, in different tartan. It looked quite striking on parade, but was not at all suitable for engaging French Canadians in rocky, thickly-wooded country. However, the 71st seem to have managed well-enough.

The 74th had embarked for the Continent in 1815, but like the 71st had been delayed by contrary winds in Cork harbour, and therefore missed the honour of fighting in

Army Museums Ogilby Trust

Colour Sergeant   *Sergeant*   *Sergeant-Major*   *Private*
71st H.L.I 1837

Wellington's final and greatest victory. Instead, they spent the next thirty years or so in Canada and the West Indies—which in those days, were so insalubrious that few soldiers returned from them. The regiment returned to Scotland in 1845, but two years later the failure of the Irish potato crop caused it to be sent over to Ireland, where a formidable force had assembled to dissuade the Irish from doing anything rash in demonstrating that they required nourishment. The 74th marched all over the southern counties but 'found nothing to contend with excepting the discomfort of almost continual rain during its field employment'.

In 1851, the various Boer 'treks' in South Africa, made in order to escape the British administration—and taxes—

Army Museums Ogilby Trust

Lt. Col. Eyre John Crabbe taking leave of the 74th. May 1846.

landed them in trouble with the Kaffirs, who lived between the Great Fish River and the Tugela. The Boer territory was protected by a chain of forts, each flying the Union Jack; for, wherever they trekked, the British flag followed them. They found this annoying in one way, but very welcome in another, for it meant that Great Britain was responsible for their defence to which, however, they contributed themselves, so that, in the face of an enemy, Boers and British fought shoulder to shoulder. The forts proving valueless in preventing Kaffir raids, and ultimatums being contemptuously disregarded, the situation gradually drifted into war.

The 74th arrived in South Africa in May, 1851, and for the next two years engaged in bush warfare in the Amatola Mountains. They were commanded by Lieutenant-Colonel John Fordyce, an officer of exceptional ability, who fell in action later in the year. Realizing that the scarlet coat was too conspicuous a garment in the bush, he ordered the retention of the canvas jackets worn by the troops on board ship which, after having been stained with the juice of mimosa berries, made a very effective camouflage. The trews of Lamont tartan were retained, for the green and white colours blended well with the local foliage. Thus clad, the 74th were nicknamed 'the tortoise warriors' by the Kaffirs, from a fancied resemblance to that reptile, which abounded in the Amatolas. There are many claimants for the invention of 'khaki', but it seems reasonably certain that the 74th were the first British regiment to wear something of the sort.

Fordyce had also trained the 74th to work in open order, controlled by bugle calls after the manner of light infantry, and this training proved invaluable when fighting the Kaffirs in the dense forests of the Amatolas.

The Kaffir War was no picnic but, like most wars, a period of hardship, heroism and horror. The Kaffirs were stalwart foes, and a vast number of small, though desperate,

Tending the wounded after the engagement at Waterkloof, October 24, 1851, after a Hottentot ambush.

engagements had to be fought before the British and Boers finally got the better of them. One of the spurs of the Amatolas, known as the Waterkloof, had to be attacked several times before the Kaffirs finally abandoned it. The first attack ended with the 74th having to withdraw down a steep, winding and narrow pass, through dense forest full of Kaffirs, throwing spears and charging in with assegais. As the 74th were in single-file, every man had to fight for himself. One soldier, with a spear through his chest, was seen to pursue the Kaffir who had thrown it and kill him with the bayonet before dying himself. Another was dragged into the bush by the straps of his equipment, but he slipped them over his shoulders and killed one Kaffir with his own assegai before being speared by the others, who were then all bayoneted by the soldier's comrades. One of the buglers, having no other means of defence, 'blew the alarm in a Kaffir's face', which caused him to fall over backwards.

In January, 1852, the *Birkenhead* sailed for the Cape with two officers and seventy-three rank and file for the 74th, and smaller drafts for nine other regiments, amounting in all to just under 500 all-ranks with their families, who mustered twenty-five women and thirty-one children. Major Seton of the 74th commanded all troops on board. The ship ran on to the rocks while rounding the Cape during the night of February 25, and was stove in just aft of the foremast, causing the troops sleeping on the lower deck to be drowned in their hammocks. All other troops were mustered on deck by Seton and his officers, and told off to the pumps and other duties, but the ship settled fast, and the women and children were put into the boats and rowed clear, for there were not enough boats for the soldiers. The ship then sank, and as she did so, the troops were paraded on the poop deck. The master then shouted 'every man for himself!' but Seton ordered the soldiers to stand fast, lest by jumping overboard they should swamp the boats with the women and children. His order was obeyed without question, and he and his officers and men went down with the ship. Seton was drowned; also Ensign Russell of the 74th, a lad of sixteen, who had been ordered into the boats with the women but either would not go or, as some say, gave up his place in the boat to a seaman. Forty-eight rank and file of the regiment were also drowned.

The *Birkenhead* disaster caused a great stir at the time for, in those days, the call 'every man for himself!' meant what it said, and although a man would naturally try to help his own wife and children, he was not expected to sacrifice himself for women and children generally. The discipline and conduct of the troops therefore excited particular admiration; the King of Prussia ordering the story to be read out at the head of each of his regiments. The '*Birkenhead* Drill', and the rule 'women and children first!' thenceforth became the established procedure in times of danger, and the 74th can claim a major share in bringing it about.

At the end of 1852 the Governor-General reported that

the Kaffir War was at an end, although the chiefs had not in fact capitulated and the Basutos, who had risen in their support, were still in the field. In November the 74th marched into Basutoland, having first received some arrears of pay, which enabled them to purchase a few extras to supplement their daily ration which 'was not sufficient of itself to maintain an able-bodied man in full exercise'. They had also to purchase veldtschoen to replace their worn-out boots; but were otherwise still wearing their tattered canvas jackets and trews, which had seen nearly two years service in the field under all sorts of weather conditions. They took everything as it came however, without either grumbles or complaints due, it seems, to the leadership and example of their officers, who shared their every danger and hardship, and looked after them as well as they could. It was found incidentally, after Colonel Fordyce's death, that he had been anonymously paying out of his own pocket for extra comforts for the soldiers' families, who had been left at Simonstown.

In the campaign in Basutoland, there was but one engagement, into which the Basutos put 7,000 horsemen, who fought with such skill and bravery that the British troops had their work cut out to get the better of them. Fighting went on all day and night before the Basutos decided they had had enough. Their chief, Moshesh, then surrendered in a dignified letter to the Governor-General, promising to keep the Queen's peace in future; a promise which he and his successors faithfully observed. The 74th left South Africa in a sailing ship in November, 1853, and landed at Madras in the following month.

An officer of the 74th Highlanders, 1853.

Chapter 4

The Crimean War and Central India Campaign

Imperial War Museum

Balaclava with a distant view of Kodi Kevy. In the foreground is the harbour.

IN MARCH, 1854, as a result of Russian aggression against Turkey, the Crimean War broke out, with Great Britain and France forced into an alliance for the protection of their common interests. The British Army at this time consisted of a collection of regiments, which were not even organized into brigades, and there were no transport or medical services. The regiments however, were of very high calibre indeed, and within the first few months they beat the Russians on the Alma and at Inkerman and Balaclava, forcing them back on their great fortress of Sevastopol. Hunger, exposure and disease then took their toll of the British forces. The whole Empire had to be combed for reinforcements, and the 71st landed in the Crimea in November, 1854, and February, 1855. The regiment at that time had two battalions, one in Canada and the other in Corfu, but after arriving in the Crimea they joined together again, to form one regiment. At this stage of the war, the operations were confined to the area round Sevastopol, which was under siege, but in May, 1855, the 71st sailed with a small expedition to capture the Straits of Kerch, at the eastern end of the Crimea, in order to cut the

Army Museums Ogilby Trust

71st Highland Light Infantry. A mounted officer in the Crimea. A photograph by Roger Fenton.

Men of the Highland Division photographed in the Crimea.

Russians' sea communications. The expedition was brilliantly successful, resulting in the expulsion of the enemy and the capture of 300 guns and five supply ships. During the rest of the war, the 71st was employed in raiding the enemy supply dumps on the shore of the sea of Azov, although one company fought with the Highland Division, and was present at the fall of Sevastopol.

After the war, the 71st were stationed in Malta, but sailed for India in January, 1858, and, a month later took the field in the Central India Campaign.

The Indian Mutiny had broken out in May of the previous year. By the time the 71st arrived it has been got under control, but large bands of rebels and mutineers were still at large in Central India, led by the Rani of Jhansi and a scoundrelly individual called Tantia Topi. The Central India Field Force, of two weak brigades commanded by Sir Hugh Rose, had therefore been formed to march from Bombay to the Jumna and establish contact with Sir Colin

Army Museums Ogilby Trust
71st Officer's Shako, 1857-62.

Campbell, the commander-in-chief, who was operating north of the river.

The 71st, dressed in loose, pyjama-like suits dyed in curry powder, joined the 2nd brigade at Koonch, where it was 'playing at long balls', with the rebels, while the 1st brigade was working round their rear. The 71st, exhausted after a long march in intense heat, had just deployed when, wrote Private James Watt, 'Sir Hugh Rose ordered up the 14th Cavalry. At it they went, their sabres gleaming in the sun. It was a fine sight to see. The enemy did not wait a moment longer, but to the right-about they went, and our fellows after them, cutting and slashing. Now came the order for us to enter, and we entered double quick, but stand they would not'. The regiment had one man wounded in this affair, but several died from heatstroke. Few days passed during the campaign without similar losses, which is not to be wondered at, when the troops were marching thirty miles a day in heat so fierce that they were often unable to ram the bullets down the barrels of their rifles, and had to get to close quarters with the bayonet. The victims were thrown into bullock-wagons, and 'an effort made to revive them', by throwing water over them at the next halt. If this did not succeed, they were reckoned to be dead, and buried by the roadside wrapped up in blankets, officers and men alike. One man, whose medals were being removed preparatory to burial, was found to be showing faint symptoms of a heart-beat and in fact, came to life again under another bucketfull of stagnant water, resuming his place in the ranks and being careful, no doubt, to avoid collapsing again.

The ruthless determination with which the British troops dealt with the mutineers, in the face of such intolerable conditions, is unprecedented. It was the result of their fury at the inhuman treatment meted out to British women and children at Cawnpore and many other isolated garrisons which had been over-run before help could reach them; the horror of their fate being emphasized by their courage and fortitude in meeting it. There was consequently no grumbling in the ranks, even those of men lately arrived in the country, at being called upon to carry out thirty mile marches at a forced pace, in a temperature of 120° in the shade, and to fight a battle at the end.

Not infrequently, when it was known that a rebel force was concentrated ahead, the pace of the advance would be regulated by the cavalry, so that the infantry would have to double. This happened in an engagement at Ranod, on the Scind River, when two companies of the 71st, accompanied by two squadrons of cavalry and a troop of the Gwalior Camel Corps, marched against a large body of rebels led by Feroz Shah. In spite of doubling, the unfortunate 71st began to lose ground, whereupon forty of them were mounted behind the camel drivers and so landed in the middle of a vast number of drugged fanatics. Several of them were cut to pieces and others lost arms and legs, but nearly 500 rebels lay dead on the field before the day ended—a far greater number than that of the entire British force engaged.

The first Victoria Cross awarded to the Highland Light Infantry was won in an action at Morar on June 16, 1858, by Private George Rodgers, who attacked and worsted seven rebels single-handed, killing six and taking one prisoner. His recommendation came from General Nicholson, who witnessed the incident. Like many other regiments at the time, the 71st disliked the idea of making special awards for gallantry in action, and declined to put any names forward. It was apparently felt—by all ranks— that to single out an individual as having been particularly brave was to hold the honour cheap of all his comrades. In this instance, General Nicholson had also wished to recommend Sergeant Ewing, who ran to the help of one of his officers who was surrounded by the enemy, and saved his life by a skilful use of the bayonet. His selfless courage certainly equalled that of Private Rodgers, but it seems that the rank and file protested that Ewing 'had done nothing more than his plain duty', whereas they grudgingly admitted that Rodgers' conduct was, possibly, a little out of the ordinary.

A sharp engagement preceded the capture of the rebel-held town of Kalpi on the Jumna, which was approached by night and attacked at dawn, with the 71st in the lead. 'The enemy appeared in front in force,' wrote Private Watt, 'and a halt was ordered, but so keen was our men to meet them that they could not be halted till the Bugle sounded three times.' The halt was to enable General Sir Hugh Rose to bring up the cavalry and guns. As soon as he had done so, 'the advance sounded again', and the rebels were driven back into the town. This was then attacked after a reconnaisance, and soon cleared of enemy, who were pursued as they fled by both cavalry and guns. By this time, 'we were all pretty nigh used up, so some lay down to sleep, consequently when they awoke they were not able to stand on their feet . . . at last a piper started up a reel, and all who could lift a leg went at it . . . this had the effect of completely arousing the sleepers, yet some had to be taken to hospital, but mostly all recovered in a few days'.

The capture of the walled city of Gwalior was a more serious affair. The 71st had been carrying out forced marches for several days, mostly by night in order to escape some of the terrific heat. 'June 16 . . . arrived at our camping ground at about 7 a.m., but just as we were going to pitch camp, an order came to form up into Brigades. We were all pretty tired, but when it became known that Gwalior was to be attacked, all fatigue was forgotten and everyone was in high spirits and eager for the fight.' The garrison of Gwalior, mostly consisting of the Maharajah's mutinous State Forces, came out to meet the British force, and were charged by cavalry, while the 71st were sent off in skirmishing order at the double to turn their right flank. They were soon heavily engaged. 'Now commenced a regular hand to hand encounter, the enemy fought for death or life, as we came close to them they threw down their firelocks and drew their tulwars. Lieutenant Neave was shot dead leading his men, by this time they were surrounded, and every man of them was shot dead or bayoneted. Now we had time to look around us, in the bottom of the nullah lay two of our men, one of them had been drawn down when making a thrust with his bayonet, the other man dashed in to save his comrade, but both were cut to pieces. The bayonet was but of little use to these desperate men, for when it was drove into them they seized it and cut at you with their tulwars, until shot down by someone. Some severe wounds were received this way.'

It must be remembered, that this action was fought out around mid-day at the hottest part of the year in India, and that the troops had been marching since midnight the day before. Nor was it the end, for Gwalior was not taken until June 20, after continuous and desperate fighting of which the above description by Private Watt is a sample.

After the capture of Gwalior, the Maharajah Scindia, who had been loyal to the British throughout the Mutiny, re-entered his capital city in state. He also inspected the 71st and 'rode up and down the ranks. He was greatly taken up with the pipes, they played a number of tunes, both quick and slow time. He seemed never to have seen or heard anything of the kind before'. To show his appreciation he invited the regiment to send a party of all-ranks, to include the pipers, to a festival held in honour of his return to Gwalior. Private Watt was there and when, at the Maharajah's request, the pipers struck up, he 'thought that his people did not like it, for some turned up their eyes in an unmistakable manner'. The Indian music however, was even less appreciated by the British soldiers: 'a number of women sat in a sort of a pitt singing a song, but heavens what a song, it reminded me of a sow's litter. Nevertheless all went home in high spirits at the Rajah's treat.'

After this, the 71st went off 'Tanti hunting', as they described the pursuit of the rebel leader Tantia Topi, which involved rushing all over Central India, mostly on their feet, but sometimes on camels. After their quarry had been caught and hanged, and the Mutiny finally surpressed, the regiment returned to Gwalior, but after a few years, during which many men were lost in cholera outbreaks, the 71st marched for the North-West Frontier, where a group of fanatical desperadoes, known as the Sittanas, who had taken refuge in the Mahaban Mountains after their expulsion from Bengal forty years earlier, were causing trouble by raiding into British India. Being Moslems, they could count on the support of the Pathan tribes, although they were not popular among the Panthans generally, so that a British and Indian force amounting to about 5,000 men of all arms had to be concentrated to deal with them.

The 71st entered the Yusufzai tribal territory in October, 1863. It being 'cold weather' in India, and getting really cold on the Frontier, they could not wear the thin khaki uniforms of the Central India Campaign and were obliged therefore, to take the field in scarlet tunics, pipe-clayed equipment and tartan; which was the only warm clothing they had—and as they were only issued with shirts and no underclothes, even that was none too warm in the bitter conditions among the mountains of the Yusufzai.

In the British and Indian armies, fighting the Pathans later became a specialized form of warfare for which the troops were previously trained, but in those days, British soldiers were expected to be capable of engaging and defeating any kind of enemy, under any conditions and in every conceivable sort of country—mountains, forests, deserts, plough or arable. And, as a matter of fact, so they could and did, exhibiting a tough resolution and powers of adaptability which is difficult to comprehend and appreciate in modern times.

The only other British regiment with the Sittana Expedition was the 101st, old comrades of the 71st, who had shared the honours of Porto Novo seventy years before. A minor incident early in the campaign further cemented the mutual regard which the two regiments had for one another. Captain Smith of the 71st was withdrawing from a picquet position when he was shot in the leg and left on the ground unnoticed by his men, in the face of a mass of advancing enemy swordsmen. Lieutenant Chapman of the 101st went to his assistance and refused to abandon him, so that the two officers were cut to pieces together. The 71st repaid the debt some days later, when a company of the 101st was overrun during a Pathan attack on a picquet position known as the Crag Picquet. The position, on the summit of a lofy eminence, was occupied by several thousand of the enemy, who cut up the unfortunate survivors of the 101st and threw their heads down the slope, in full view of the main camp. It was immediately counter-attacked by the 71st, who advanced up the hill in open

74th Highlanders, 1866.

column of companies, with pipes playing, The Pathans were in no hurry to depart, and were caught at the bayonet-point by the 71st, who were all infuriated by the disaster which had overtaken the 101st, so that a massive slaughter ensued which did not cease until every Pathan had been hunted out of cover and the whole ridge cleared. The whole affair was, in fact, so impressive that the Pathans made no further attacks and capitulated shortly afterwards. The 71st, who had suffered some sixty casualties during the campaign, including their commanding-officer, received the personal congratulations of the Commander-in-Chief of India.

The 74th, who had returned to India after the Kaffir War, were not at first called out for the suppression of the Indian Mutiny, for they were engaged against the Moplahs in Southern India, and having some very tough experiences in the process. Private Joseph Park, for example, was given every reason for agreeing with Private Watts' disparaging remarks on the use of the bayonet when dealing with fanatics—who were often drugged. He had driven his bayonet through one Moplah who, although he dropped dead later, was first able to cut Park's throat from ear to ear. Park however, proved to be tougher than his opponent, for he survived to win many a drink by exhibiting his ghastly wound in the pubs at home. The Mutiny as such, was over by the time the 74th had dealt with the Moplahs, but the regiment was sent to keep order among its old enemies the Mahrattas, and lost a dozen men during the capture of the forts of Kopal and Noorgund, which were garrisoned by rebels.

Returning home in 1864, the 74th became involved in the 'Fenian Riots' in Ireland, and were afterwards stationed in Gibraltar, Malaya and Hong Kong, before marching into Maryhill Barracks—then in the country outside Glasgow—in January, 1880. Three months later the 71st after being stationed in Edinburgh, Ireland and Cyprus returned to Edinburgh and garrisoned the castle.

Band of the 71st Highland Light Infantry, Malta, 1870.

Chapter 5

The Small Wars

1881 SAW the introduction of the 'Cardwell Reforms', which, in brief, reorganized the Army into two-battalion regiments by pairing off the existing single-battalion regiments; the object being to have one battalion at home and the other abroad—although it seldom worked out that way. The 71st were accordingly paired with the 74th, and the two regiments re-designated the 1st and 2nd Battalions, The Highland Light Infantry. The amalgamation was reasonably successful, although the new battalions never forgot their old numbers and continued to refer to themselves unofficially as the 71st and 74th; while half a century was to elapse before officers exchanged freely from one to the other.

At the time of the Reforms, the Highland regiments were given the opportunity of returning to the kilt, which most had discarded during the Napoleonic wars. All of them accepted except the H.L.I., whose officers felt it to be inappropriate for a light infantry regiment. The intention to dress the Lowland regiments in tartan trews was unfortunately not known when this decision was made, and the result was, that being dressed in the same uniforms as the Lowland regiments caused the H.L.I. to be regarded in the public mind as a Lowland Regiment, in spite of its name and traditions. Furthermore, the establishment of the Highland and Lowland military districts, by adopting the Forth and Clyde as a boundary, meant that Glasgow, whose citizens were more Highland than Lowland, became part of the Lowland District. This eventually led to the

Territorial battalions of the H.L.I. being incorporated in the 52nd Lowland Division, instead of the 51st Highland Division.

However, over a year after becoming the 2nd Battalion of the Highland Light Infantry, the 74th marched with the Highland Brigade to Ramleh, still wearing their old Lamont tartan, scarlet tunics and pipe-clayed equipment. Their only concession to the heat of the Egyptian desert was the 'Wolseley' helmet, and, for the first time in history, what were to become the very well-known initials, H.L.I., took the place of numerals on their shoulder-straps. They were in Egypt in order to crush a rebellion led by Colonel Arabi Pasha against the Khedive Tewfik, and restore law and order to a country which had become of vital national interest to the British Imperial Government.

Nothing much happened at Ramleh, and the Highland Brigade was moved to Ismailia, Arabi Pasha having constructed strong, fortified lines at Tel-el-Kebir, for the protection of the approaches to Cairo. In September the British force, commanded by Sir Garnet Wolseley, marched against him, and on the night of the twelfth, the Highland Brigade formed up 'in line of column of double companies by half battalions', and sat down in the sand to enjoy a tot of rum. The Brigade was formed up with the 42nd on the right, the 75th and 79th Highlanders in the centre, and the 74th, who were to direct, on the left. A star was pointed out to the commanding-officer, Colonel Abel Straghan to march by. 'I can almost see the star now,' he wrote later, 'the second from the left of a constellation of four, due west, and at that time right over Kebir.'

Unnoticed by the Egyptians, the Highland Brigade arrived before the fortifications just as dawn was breaking. The enemy then opened fire, and the order to fix bayonets was given as their bullets sang through the air, 'like wild-fowl flighting'. The bugles sounded the charge, and the pipers struck up, as the 74th rushed forward, 'crouching a little, but there was none of that ducking which is supposed to occur with troops the first time under fire'. The enemy positions however, were covered by a very deep and wide ditch, and in the uncertain light, the leading companies of the 74th fell into it, leaving the support companies exposed to a murderous fire at close range. The Major, two other officers and some fifty rank and file had fallen, before the support companies could get into a position for volley-firing, under cover of which, those in the ditch were able to clamber out and carry the enemy defences at the bayonet-point. When dawn broke, the whole Egyptian Army was on the run, pursued by the British cavalry and guns. Four days later the 74th marched into Cairo and hoisted the Union Jack over the Citadel, where it remained flying for some seventy years. The regiment—or battalion rather—had lost three officers and eighteen rank and file killed, and five officers and fifty-four rank and file wounded; the heaviest casualties of any regiment engaged. The Victoria Cross was awarded to Lieutenant Edwards, for the gallantry with which he led his platoon into an enemy redoubt, and there were numerous other decorations received, including

Army Museums Ogilby Trust

Officers of the 74th Highlanders in 1880.

several Egyptian awards, given by the grateful Khedive.

1884 found the 74th—the overseas battalion—at Rawalpindi, awaiting an expected invasion of India by the Russians; while the 71st—the home battalion—were engaged on the old chore of trying to keep the peace in Ireland. The Russians having changed their minds, the 74th were left in peace until Sunday, July 31, 1897, when the battalion was at Cawnpore with all the officers except one on leave, and orders came to mobilize immediately. Within twenty-four hours, the battalion was in the train for the North-West Frontier. At Lucknow, it was joined by its invalids who, on hearing that the 74th were off once more for the wars, had left their beds in the hospital and slipped on to the train unnoticed. When discovered, they were clapped up in the guard's van under arrest by a horrified Adjutant who, however, relented later and let them out. 'Have to admire the damn fellers' spirit,' he remarked.

At Rawalpindi, the 74th joined the Malakand Field Force, under Sir Bindon Blood, and spent the next twelve months fighting the Pathans. It was very hard work, during which the 74th became increasingly irritated by the refusal of the tribesmen to stand and fight, so that they were put to great inconvenience to no apparent purpose. However, '*patience*' remarked Private Boyle. 'Remember Job.' Any soldier worth his salt could make himself comfortable, even on a frontier campaign in the middle of the hot weather. 'Get a couple of sacks, rip up the sides, put them on your uprights, make friends with the cook and bakery wallahs, and if you don't spend a pretty good time of it, well, you need your nurse again.'

Actually, the 74th were in action many times, opening fire by company volleys at ranges of about 1,400 yards. The fire was too accurate for the Pathans' liking, and the only time the 74th could get to close quarters was at the taking of the Tanga Pass when, 'the hill was steep,' wrote Boyle, 'and our progress necessarily slow. The enemy did not waste their ammunition they reserved their fire until we were well up. We advanced as ordered, our Colonel showing very prominently at the head of our regiment.' The Pass was carried at the bayonet-point, and the Pathans fled, after which, 'our pipers played, we gave a cheer, then we fell out to eat our bully beef and biscuits, and have a good drink from our water bottles'.

After the capture of the Tanga Pass the Pathans surrendered, and the 74th spent some months quartered in various of their villages; expressing the opinion that 'if the Pathans had shown half so much perseverance as the bugs, they would have driven us out of the country'. The battalion spent its last year in India, 1895, at Karachi, preparatory to leaving for Ceylon. Before it left it won the premier football tournament in India—the Durand Trophy —for the fifth time in all and the third time in succession, thus retaining it in perpetuity. A regulation-size silver football, mounted on a plinth, it has been a prized possession of the regiment ever since.

While the 74th were thus engaged in beating the Pathans on the battlefield, and all comers on the football field, their 'home battalion' the 71st, had moved from Ireland, first to Malta and then to Crete. The latter island, which was inhabited by Christian descendants of the Venetians and Mohammedan descendants of Turkish pirates, was in a state of unrest fostered by Greece in order to provide an excuse for taking it over from the Turks. This idea was not favoured by the great powers of Europe, and an international force was sent to keep the peace. The Turkish authorities in the island objected to this interference in their affairs, and their resentment came to a head in 1898 when Colonel Reid of the 71st was ordered to take over the Turkish tax office, collect the taxes himself, and use the money for the expenses of the international force. The Bashi Bazooks— armed Turkish irregulars—rose without warning and attacked the camp and picquets of the 71st, who were taken by surprise, for they had established very friendly relations with the Turks, whom they greatly preferred to the Greeks. However, although surprised, and being forbidden to open fire in their own defence, they soon succeeded in re-establishing law and order—though at a cost of an officer and nine men killed and twenty-five wounded. No help was forthcoming from the other units of the international brigade, who kept well out of the way until the rising was crushed, when they provided soldiers for the international firing-squads at the executions of the leaders of the revolt, after they had been sentenced by an international court.

The services of the 71st on this occasion received official recognition in the form of an unusual number of honours and awards—thirty-two in all—far greater than were normally given for a whole campaign. In fact, the 74th went through the whole Malakand Campaign without getting a single award, even for the capture of the Tanga Pass. The discipline, steadiness and sheer cold courage exhibited by the 71st in the face of vast numbers of Moslem fanatics, when they were not allowed to open fire, was, however, quite outstanding. Their spirit can best be recalled by the words of Private John Bell when, as he was dying of his wounds, he was asked if he had any last message: 'just tell ma mither I deed daeing ma duty'.

The 71st—still, it will be rememberd, the 'Home' battalion of the H.L.I.—were not given long to lick the wounds received in Crete. On October 11, 1899, war was declared against Great Britain by the Boer Republics, and the 71st, who had only landed at Plymouth a few months previously, sailed from that port for the Cape on the twenty-third, and a month later joined the Highland Brigade before Magersfontein. The Boers had taken up positions north of the Modder River, to stop Lord Methuen from marching to the relief of Kimberley. Unknown to Lord Methuen, they had changed their defensive tactics from lying along the tops of hills to occupying trenches along the bottom, protected by barbed wire. When therefore, he made a dawn attack on December 11, he was given a rude surprise at the expense of the unfortunate Highland Brigade which led the attack.

The Highland Brigade advanced through pouring rain in pitch darkness, with the Black Watch leading, followed by the Seaforth and Argylls, who were to deploy to right and left of the Watch. The H.L.I. formed the second line, in reserve. The Boers opened fire at short range just as the three leading regiments were deploying, and threw them into confusion. A charge was attempted, but frustrated by the wire. The H.L.I. had just been ordered to lie down, when the rest of the Brigade swept over them in disorder, and many officers and men received severe kicks on the head. When dawn broke, the Brigade rallied, and spent the day trying to get forward, aided by attacks which Methuen put in on the flanks. It was all to no avail, and in the evening Methuen drew back to the Modder River. The 71st lost two officers and fourteen rank and file killed, and seven officers and sixty-seven rank and file wounded. The Victoria Cross was awarded to Corporal Shaul for leading an advance across the open and saving many wounded men under close-range fire.

The 71st thus had an unfortunate introduction to the Boer War, but they thought nothing of the setback. In war, as in peace, one cannot always be successful, and it is the last battle that counts. Before the Boers capitulated 'nearly every town in Orange River Colony,' wrote Colonel Kelham, 'has heard the pipes of the H.L.I.' The battalion led the Highland Brigade at Heilbron, and into action at Retiefs Nek—a strong Boer position which it captured without assistance from the rest of the Brigade. 'The H.L.I.,' said the Brigadier, Hector MacDonald, 'are like goats among the rocks and hills.' Spitz Kop, another strong Boer position, was also attacked and captured by the 71st, with the support of the Lovat Scouts, and, after Kitchener had hemmed the Boers in by his blockhouse system there were, wrote Colonel Kelham, 'so many little fights along the Orange River that it is impossible to relate them'. About 200 of the 71st were mounted, and fought with the 12th Mounted Infantry Battalion. On one occasion, near Pretoria, they had the unusual experience for infantrymen, of engaging the enemy on horseback, neither side having had time to dismount. They got the best of it after quite a fierce encounter, during which their leader, Captain Browne, lost an arm.

Chapter 6

The Great War

THE 71st did not return home after the Boer War, for during it the 74th came back from India and became the 'home' battalion, furnishing drafts for the 71st in South Africa. The 71st went on to Egypt, the Sudan, and India, while the 74th travelled between the Channel Islands, Edinburgh and Aldershot. In 1908, the Territorial Army was raised out of the old Volunteers, and the Militia was redesignated the Special Reserve. In the H.L.I., the Militia became the 3rd and 4th Battalions (Special Reserve), and the Volunteers became the 5th, 6th, 7th, 8th and 9th (Glasgow Highlanders) H.L.I. (T.A.). By this time it had become apparent that Great Britain would be obliged to fight Germany, sooner or later, and, to meet this threat, the Regular Army at home was organized into an Expeditionary Force of six infantry and one cavalry divisions which, with the help of the French and reinforcements from the Dominions, India and the Colonies, was optimistically reckoned to be sufficient to deal with Germany on the Continent, while the Territorials dealt with any invasion of Great Britain which the enemy might be misguided enough to attempt.

War with Germany was declared on August Bank Holiday, 1914. The Regular Army mobilized with extraordinary speed and efficiency, and on August 24, a cavalry division and the first four infantry divisions were in action at Mons. The 74th, who were covering the exits from the mining town of Paturages, had no difficulty in holding up the German hordes advancing against them. Like the rest of the British Expeditionary Force which, though minute in size by Continental standards, was the best fighting formation the world has ever seen, they had been trained to fire fifteen well-aimed rounds a minute from their short Lee-Enfields; while their skill with the bayonet was superlative: long point, short point and jab, butt stroke, slash and boot; gallantry and confidence; the fighting spirit; they had them all.

However, the French pulled out, so the unbeaten British army had to go too. The retreat from Mons was followed by the Battle of the Marne, which halted the German advance, and the 74th were then moved over to Ypres. Nothing dismayed them, but they had become seriously angry over the unsportsmanlike tricks played by the Germans, for which their previous experiences against decent fellows like the Kaffirs, Boers and Pathans had quite unprepared them. Such tricks as dressing up in French uniforms, for instance, and, worse still, holding up their hands in surrender and then reopening fire. This happened on the Verneuil Ridge, where Sir Archibald Gibson-Craig was shot dead, sword in hand, when leading his platoon against a mass of Germans standing with their hands up. But his platoon saw to it that they paid for this cold-blooded murder to the last man. Also on the Verneuil Ridge, the first V.C. for the 74th in the war was won by a reservist, Private George Wilson, who slaughtered an enemy machine-gun team of an officer and six men, and captured the gun all by himself.

By the end of the First Battle of Ypres there was not much left of the 74th—or of the British Expeditionary Force—but the enemy had been fought to a standstill, the Channel Ports had been saved, and reinforcements were on their way. Within two months of the outbreak of war, the H.L.I. had no fewer than seventeen battalions on a war footing: four Special Reserve—the 3rd, 4th, 13th and 14th —five Territorial battalions, and six of Kitchener's new Special Service battalions. Towards the end of First Ypres the first Indian contingent arrived in the field and with it the 71st, in the Lahore Division. Meanwhile Lieutenant W. L. Brodie had won another V.C. for the 74th in what he described as 'a bit of a scrap'. The Germans attacking suddenly had overrun his two machine-guns, whereupon he seized a rifle and killed nine of them, five with the bullet and four with the bayonet. He then got one of the guns into action just as an H.L.I. company charged in using bayonets, butts, boots and fists. By the end of it there were eighty Germans dead on the field, and fifty-four prisoners. The 74th lost fifteen killed and twenty-six wounded in this affair.

One of the first Territorial battalions to arrive in the field was the 9th H.L.I. (Glasgow Highlanders) which joined the 5th Infantry Brigade at Bailleul on November 23, 1914. In December the 71st met the 74th at Givenchy —the first time the two old regiments had met within the sound of the guns since Seringapatam. Neither was any more a Regular Army battalion, except in name. Their first and second reinforcements had long been used up and only a few old regulars, officers and men, remained to hand on the regimental spirit and traditions to the half-trained special reservists and raw recruits who had followed them. Throughout the horrible winter the two battalions fought alongside one another in the trenches before Festubert, but only the 71st went into action at the Battle of Neuve Chapelle in March, losing in one day eight officers killed and four wounded, and nearly 250 rank and file.

At the beginning of April 1915, the British took over the vulnerable Ypres Salient from the French, just before the enemy attacked. The Second Battle of Ypres developed and raged for a week before the 71st entered. By the time the enemy attacks petered out at the end of the month, the battalion had lost five officers and 282 rank and file, but a couple of Second-Lieutenants and 139 men had joined while the battalion was actually in action.

At this time there was no pause in the fighting. As soon

as the German attacks had been halted, the British counter-attacked, and the Battles of Aubers Ridge and Festubert followed, with horrible slaughter and among scenes of such confusion that an officer of the 74th, who were marching forward to relieve the 52nd, was heard to remark that he hoped they would not relieve the Germans instead! At Festubert, the 74th were relieved by the 71st, after losing eleven officers and 371 rank and file, while the 71st lost seven officers and 120 rank and file in the one day, after taking over. No material advantage was gained by either side as a result of these desperate and prolonged encounters, which only terminated when the ammunition ran out. But the British got somewhat the best of it, although everything was against them, and their fantastic gallantry and determination had a considerable moral effect on the enemy, whose previous arrogance slowly gave way to doubts and fears.

In October 1914, the German warships, *Goeben* and *Bresaau*, accompanied by a Turkish squadron, bombarded the Russian ports of Odessa and Sebastopol. This led to an immediate declaration of war on Turkey by the Allies, and two British attempts were made to seize the Dardanelles. The first was a purely naval affair which proved that the enterprise was impossible without troops. An Expeditionary Force was then landed on the Gallipoli Peninsula in April, 1915, and, as the Turks were then on the alert, a static situation developed, similar to that on the Western Front, in which vast bloodshed and suffering achieved no useful results. The 52nd Lowland Division left Scotland in May, 1915, and landed on the Gallipoli Peninsula in July. The 157th Infantry Brigade of this Division was composed of the 5th, 6th and 7th T.A. battalions of the H.L.I. and the 5th Argylls, and was known as the H.L.I. Brigade. The officers and men possessed in full measure, the same attributes of gallantry and determination as their comrades on the Western Front, but they were still only civilians in uniform, with but a rudimentary knowledge of military affairs. The corpses with which the field was littered, and the arms and legs sticking out of the walls of their trenches filled them with 'an emotion of inexpressible horror', but in no way weakened their resolve to teach the Turk a thing or two about fighting. 'Major Fisher, commanding the 2nd Royal Fusiliers, was good enough to let us have a perusal of his *Trench Standing Orders*. Afterwards he allowed Captain Simson to make a copy of these. They proved invaluable to us.' This manual was studied within short range of the enemy positions, by amateur soldiers who had never before been under fire, on the eve of a Divisional attack.

The attack, in which all three H.L.I. battalions were engaged, was designed to capture part of the enemy network of trenches before Achi Baba. It was preceded by an intense bombardment which seemed, to the soldiers awaiting the order to advance, to have completely destroyed their objectives. When however, they attacked through the dense clouds of smoke and dust which had been raised, they found the Turks still very much alive, so that they had to leap down upon them and get busy with the bayonet. As the enemy was driven back from trench to trench, they hurled hand-grenades. The H.L.I. had not been issued with these, so they picked up the Turkish grenades, with the fuses still smouldering, and flung them back, regardless of the fact that many exploded in the hand.

'A man,' said Napoleon, 'learns quickly on the battlefield.' So indeed he does, if he manages to stay alive. So many of the Territorial Army and Service Battalions were killed while learning the business of war in these desperate affairs, and being replaced by yet more raw recruits, that it was never possible for the units to reach the standard of the pre-war Regular Army. Except, that is, in the qualities of courage and endurance, which they never lacked, and never lost. The enterprise at Gallipoli was abandoned in January, 1916, after all attempts to throw the Turks out of the peninsula had proved fruitless. The last action fought by the H.L.I. Brigade was in December, 1915, in what was known as the Eski Line, and the Brigade was among the last troops to be evacuated. Morale remained as high as ever, and the Turks had not seen the last of the H.L.I., who were transferred to Egypt and fought at Romani, El Arish and Gaza; marched with Allenby to Jerusalem, and helped in the final eviction of the enemy from the Holy Land across the Auja. Then, in April, 1918, they were transferred to the Western Front; a move which they welcomed as offering the chance for some home leave; although they left Palestine with some regret, reflecting that 'in between the battles the life was often very pleasant'.

In another 'side-show', the Mesopotamia Campaign, the H.L.I. were represented by the 71st, who arrived off the Persian Gulf in January, 1916, from the Western Front. Exchanging their first shots with the enemy before Hanna, they fought their way right up the Tigris until, on October 30, 1918, they led into the final victory at Sharquat. Disease and battle-casualties had by that time reduced their strength to about 150 all-ranks. After leaving a company with the Army of Occupation the remainder—about forty or so—went to India, where they were immediately employed dealing with riots, after which, they were sent off to the Third Afghan War which however, was successfully terminated before they could get to it.

On the Western Front, the Battle of Festubert had been succeeded by a period of comparative quiet, with the Allies preparing a major attack against the immense salient which the German advances had created. This attack, known as the Battle of Loos, was launched on September 25, 1915, by which time Kitchener's New Army Divisions had poured into the field; among them being the 10th, 11th and 12th H.L.I., bringing the total H.L.I. battalions in action up to eight. At Loos it was the newly-arrived 12th H.L.I. which had the hardest time. Fighting in the 15th

Scottish Division, this battalion captured six guns and came out of action on September 27 having lost in killed, wounded and missing, twenty-one officers and 532 rank and file. The missing totalled 182, but only sixteen of these were reported prisoners of war, so that all the rest must either have been killed or died of wounds.

These grievous losses in no way hindered recruiting. It was arms and equipment that were short, not men. In Glasgow, the 15th H.L.I. was raised in fifteen hours out of tramways employees, one of whom remarked that, if it had not been for all the red tape, fifteen minutes would have been sufficient. Similarly, the 16th H.L.I. was raised from the Boys' Brigade, and the 17th by the Glasgow Chamber of Commerce. These three battalions all proved themselves in the Battle of the Somme, which opened on July 1, 1916, having been preceded by a trench raid carried out by the Glasgow Highlanders, which was so successful that the battalion was complimented by Sir Douglas Haig himself, who also wrote 'a most charming letter' to the Lord Provost about it.

The Battle of the Somme was, in fact, a series of battles, commencing with the Battle of Albert. It was fought to gain possession of one of the strongest parts of the German line, known as the Leipzig Redoubt, and the 15th, 16th and 17th H.L.I., in the trenches before Thiepval, all went into the attack. The 16th H.L.I. came up against intact wire, untouched by the bombardment, and lost nineteen officers and 492 rank and file within a few hours. The 17th H.L.I. had more luck, and carried the Redoubt itself but, when pressing on, they lost twenty-two officers and 447 rank and file on the second line. Retiring to the Leipzig Redoubt, they held it against repeated counter-attacks, during which Sergeant James Turnbull displayed such exceptional valour as to be awarded the V.C.—posthumously. The 15th H.L.I., who had been in reserve, were two days late in entering They then went into the Leipzig Redoubt—a pulverized

Fricourt on the Somme, 1916. Mr. Ben Tillett visits men of the H.L.I.

mass of rubble—and after desperate fighting at close quarters defeated an enemy counter-attack and killed all Germans in the second line beyond. In the one day, they lost thirteen officers and 272 rank and file.

As the British offensive continued on the Somme, all the ten H.L.I. battalions on the Western Front went into action. The latest to arrive in France was the 18th—a 'Bantam' battalion composed of men under five feet three inches in height. The Glasgow Highlanders lost 421 all-ranks at High Wood, but fought on until within six weeks their casualties had mounted to thirty-three officers and 750 men, which was just about all they had. They were reinforced by 355 men drawn from four other Scottish regiments, of whom, 'some were very young, some rather old, and some were just out of hospital'. But they went on fighting. So did all the others go on fighting, day after day, week after week, in conditions which the devil himself could scarcely improve on in hell. The 74th and 18th H.L.I. at Delville Wood, the 10th/11th H.L.I. (now amalgamated into one battalion) and 12th H.L.I. at Martinpuich, the 15th H.L.I. at Orvillers, all suffered similar casualties, and had either been reorganized into two companies or heavily reinforced by all sorts of people, so that they had become barely recognizable. By the autumn the battlefield had become such a sea of mud that men and animals were sometimes swallowed up in it; but there was still no let-up, although when the Battle of the Ancre commenced in November, it had begun to snow.

Struggling through snow and sleet, the 16th and 17th H.L.I. advanced together against the Redan Ridge at dawn on November 18. The whole of the 17th and the right company of the 16th were decimated by machine-gun and rifle fire. But the survivors pressed on into the German Munich and Frankfurt trenches, overcame all resistance with the bayonet and sent back fifty prisoners. Attacks on either side having failed, the remnants of the 16th H.L.I., about 100 men under a sergeant-major, then became isolated in the Frankfurt trench, which they held for eight days. At the end of it there were only fifteen left, who were taken prisoner because they had become so weak from lack of food that they could no longer stand up. The 16th H.L.I. were awarded thirty-three decorations for this affair.

Taking a leaf out of the Duke of Wellington's book the Germans had constructed the 'Hindenburgh Line' a most formidable defensive system, behind which they intended to organize an offensive powerful enough to split the British and French armies and defeat them separately. They retired to this line in February, 1917, going back as much as thirty miles in some places. This introduced a period of open warfare during which the forward British units had to advance with advanced and flank guards out, and to deploy into orthodox formations which only the surviving regulars properly understood. Furthermore, the field artillery could not keep up across the waterlogged ground, so that they had often to go into action without artillery support, although they did get some protection from the cavalry, which rode ahead and discovered the enemy rear-guard and covering positions.

During this fighting, the 17th H.L.I. distinguished themselves at the capture of Savy, on April 1, losing 103 all-ranks on that day. The 15th H.L.I. captured a battery of six guns before Selency, in an action in which Major F. W. Lumsden, commanding the 17th H.L.I., received the V.C., but this achievement was surpassed on April 9 by the 10th/11th and 12th H.L.I. who assaulted and captured no fewer than thirty-six guns, when attacking with the 46th Brigade east of Arras.

The Battle of Arras, into which these operations developed, consisted of numerous noteworthy engagements in many of which one or other of the H.L.I. battalions took part. After the village of Monchy le Preux had been galloped by the 10th Hussars and Essex Yeomanry on April 11, it was the 10th/11th H.L.I. which took and held it against the counter-attack, while at the capture of Fayet, before St. Quentin, the 16th H.L.I. were first into the village, taking 150 prisoners and two machine-guns. On April 26 the 74th lost their commanding-officer, fourteen other officers and 269 rank and file in killed and wounded. At the same time, the 10th/11th H.L.I. and 12th H.L.I. were decimated while advancing beyond Monchy le Preux, and the Glasgow Highlanders lost 297 out of a total strength of 496 at Croisilles—but they went into action again two days later and lost another thirty-three all-ranks.

After the offensive at Arras had petered out, another was planned in Flanders to which six of the H.L.I. battalions were transferred, but they arrived too late to take part in the Battle of Messines. The 16th and 17th H.L.I. were soon in action however, repelling a German counter-attack at Nieuport, and shortly afterwards the 10th/11th and 12th H.L.I. fought in the Battle of Pilcken Ridge. The Battle of Langemarch followed, and then an attack on Cheluveldt, in which the Glasgow Highlanders lost eight officers and about 450 rank and file, and the Victoria Cross was awarded to Lance-Corporal John Hamilton for carrying supplies of ammunition and because, 'his splendid example of fearlessness and devotion to duty inspired all who saw him with fresh confidence and renewed their determination to hold on at all costs'.

Then the 15th, 16th and 17th H.L.I. went into the Third Battle of Ypres, or 'Passchendaele' as it was more usually called; fought out across a dreary waste of liquid mud, covered with waterlogged craters and shell-holes, corpses of men and animals, overturned waggons and gun-carriages; where the shelling never ceased by day or night.

The Flanders offensive having been brought to a standstill, not by the enemy but by the mud, another was immediately launched at Cambrai. Here the 14th H.L.I., which had been raised at Hamilton in July, 1915, went into battle for the first time at Bourlon Wood, where things became so confused that every man had to fight for himself, as at Inkerman. The enemy was thrown out of the wood at bayonet-point, and driven through Bourlon village, but here the 14th H.L.I. got cut off and surrounded. They were down to about eighty all-ranks, with their commanding-officer killed and 450 other casualties. Having fought on until their ammunition was exhausted, the survivors were taken prisoner.

Also at Bourlon were the 74th who, before going into action, had been ordered to leave behind their commanding-officer and a proportion of all-ranks as first reinforcement. This order was the result of the prevailing heavy losses among Lieutenant-Colonels commanding, whose experience made them difficult to replace, but it was an odd sort of order to give, nonetheless. The Battalion became involved in some very hard fighting in part of the Hindenburgh Line along the Canal du Nord, but escaped with the comparatively light casualties of about 100 all-ranks due, apparently, to the fact that it had just completed a period of intensive training.

The last German offensive of the war opened on March 21, 1918. It was on so vast a scale, with eight battalions to the half-mile and forty German Divisions to fifteen British, that it is no wonder the enemy should have been confident of driving the British into the sea. Although however, things looked grave for a while, and Sir Douglas Haig issued his famous 'Backs to the Wall', order, the morale of the British soldiers never weakened—although many were young conscripts—and the advance was halted in due course.

The blow was aimed at the line held by the British 3rd and 5th Armies, and it so happened that none of the H.L.I. battalions was in front on the opening day. The 74th was the first of them to go into action, when the battalion was ordered to cover the retirement near Berlincourt on March 22. Thereafter they fought without respite until the end of March, often cut off and seldom getting more than an hour or two's sleep at a time. But they marched through Ivergny with their pipes playing and drums beating, apparently, though very battle-worn in appearance, in the highest spirits.

Shortly after the 74th opened fire at Berlincourt, the 10th/11th and 14th H.L.I. entered at Bullecourt. They had large numbers of recruits, just arrived from home, who kept standing up 'to get a shot at Fritz'. They did not have quite such a hard time of it as the 74th, and after fighting in two major engagements at Mory and Sapigny came out of action on March 27.

The 12th and 18th H.L.I. went into action at Hardecourt,

Imperial War Museum

Bivouac of the 12th H.L.I. on the Menin Road, October 1918. In the background French Cavalry pass along the road.

after two nights in the train and a seventeen mile march. A defensive position had been formed between Hardecourt and the Somme and on it, during March 24 and 25, 'the 35th Division put up a magnificent fight against five German Divisions'. During this fighting Lieutenant-Colonel W. H. Anderson, commanding the 12th H.L.I., led a bayonet charge against the masses of advancing enemy and drove them back nearly a mile. He had already distinguished himself by leading a counter-attack which secured seventy prisoners and twelve machine-guns, and so was awarded the V.C.—posthumous, for he had fallen at the head of his battalion.

The British retirement before the German onslaught was a fighting withdrawal, in which the enemy was made to pay dearly for every yard of ground. It was marked by innumerable local British counter-attacks, of which the capture of

Ayette by the 15th H.L.I. at the beginning of April is a good example. It was launched at two o'clock in the morning, against very strong opposition, and cost the H.L.I. nearly 200 casualties. Not only did they have to fight their way through the enemy defences, but having done so, had to clear the whole village at the bayonet-point under nightmare conditions in which fresh Germans were continually pouring out of cellars and fortified houses in their rear. Their effort was rewarded by over forty decorations for gallantry.

During the Battle of the Lys, on April 9, the 40th Division, which had already suffered losses of up to seventy per cent of its strength, had to be sent in to stop an enemy breakthrough. After two days, the whole Division had been reduced to two composite battalions, among whose personnel were the survivors of the 10th/11th and 14th H.L.I., which had ceased to exist as such, having gone down fighting. If however they may still be included in the roll, though composed of dead men, there were now eleven H.L.I. battalions in action on the Western Front, for the H.L.I. Brigade had arrived from Palestine. Only the 71st were absent, fighting their way up the Tigris beyond Bagdad.

Sheer exhaustion eventually caused the British line to crumble in many places. The Glasgow Highlanders, holding a position at Neuve Englise, were joined by parties of exhausted stragglers from a dozen regiments. One of them, was led by a Sergeant-Major, who said that his men were so done-up as to be useless on their own, but that if a 'Jock' could be placed between each pair of them, they would hold on all right. But the Glasgow Highlanders did not have many Jocks left, at that time.

The enemy, however, was becoming equally exhausted and, having advanced to within forty miles of Paris, could go no further. The Allied counter-offensive was then launched in August, when the 74th went into action at The Battle of Albert. Their commanding-officer,

Lieutenant-Colonel W. L. Brodie, V.C., was killed, but the battalion captured Behagnies, a large number of prisoners, and six guns. Then the 5th, 6th and 7th H.L.I. from Palestine advanced from Ficheux and carried all before them as far as Cambrai. The 14th and 15th H.L.I. attacked across the Somme to near Brie, capturing many prisoners and guns. Day after day, week after week, the pounding went on and there was no let-up. In the Targelle Valley, the Glasgow Highlanders attacked in thick fog, losing touch with their Brigade, suffering heavy casualties from flanking fire, and eventually, becoming surrounded, having to fight their way back again. The next morning they again attacked, over ground covered with their own dead and wounded, to find the enemy gone. Near Moeuvres, the 5th H.L.I., reduced to a third of its strength, was over-run by the enemy but held its ground in numerous small posts. One of these was held by Corporal D. F. Hunter with six men in a shell-hole for three days without food or water, and with four of the men wounded. He was promoted to Sergeant and awarded the V.C., while each of his men received the Distinguished Conduct Medal.

In September, the Hindenburg Line was broken at Cambrai, after a series of battles in which the 74th, 5th, 6th and 7th H.L.I. all took part. By this time they were down to a couple of hundred men apiece, as were the Glasgow Highlanders who, when crossing the Selle and moving forward to the Sambre, were reduced to 173 all-ranks. The 74th had reached the village of Villers Pol when, on November 11, 1918, news was received of the signing of the Armistice, and the pipes and drums played up and down the village street. First into the field, the 74th were destined to be the last out of it, being detailed to the Army of Occupation. Having sent home for their colours, they crossed the frontier into Germany on December 9, marching past their Brigadier at Malmedy, who sent the following message:

'My congratulations to the 74th Highlanders on crossing

the enemy frontier to-day as a result of the battles they have fought this year. It will always be a source of pride to me to have had such a fine Scottish Regiment in the Brigade under my command, and to have saluted their colours in enemy territory.'

In the Great War, the H.L.I. fought in France, Belgium, the Dardanelles, Egypt, Palestine and Mesopotamia, taking part in sixty-four major engagements and losing in dead 598 officers and 9,428 rank and file.

Terrible casualties, hardship and suffering are no strangers to the British Army. Nevertheless, in no other conflict in its history, had it been so severely tested as in the Great War; for there was no pause in the horror for over four years. In the words of Sir Douglas Haig, 'with our backs to the wall and believing in the justice of our cause', the British soldiers, unlike those of any other nation engaged, never lost heart from start to finish. It is sad indeed, that so noble an example of what British manhood can accomplish in the defeat of tyranny and aggression, should have been lost in a subsequent wave of pacifism, and among squalid attempts to find scapegoats out of the military leaders, in order to satisfy the uneasy consciences of those who had stayed at home.

Chapter 7

The Second World War

THE BOLSHEVIK revolution of 1917 had been succeeded by a counter-revolution during the following year, which had been supported by the Allies with arms and small contingents of troops. Once Germany had been defeated however, the Allies no longer felt inclined to interfere with the internal policies of Russia, and decided to withdraw all support for the counter-revolutionary White Russians. The British contingents were at Archangel and Murmansk and, in order to withdraw them 'without disaster and without dishonour', as Mr. Winston Churchill put it, it was considered necessary to reinforce them as a preliminary. The 74th were among the reinforcements dispatched, and sailed off to Archangel in high spirits, only too ready 'to have a bash at the Bolos', and landed on August 26. There followed a somewhat dreary experience, lasting until October, during which they were deployed over hundreds of miles of country in various small posts. One platoon, sent to a village called Kolvetsky, on the shores of the White Sea, was ambushed in its boats, while putting in to land, and lost ten men killed without getting a chance to fight back. Otherwise, there was little excitement, although the battalion was quite sorry to leave the country, in which they had established very friendly relations with the inhabitants, whom they were distressed to have to abandon to the inhumanities practised by the Bolsheviks.

Home from Russia, the 74th were immediately sent to Ireland, where the rebellion was in full swing. The battalion was deployed into ten detachments spread over the southern counties, but was then called in again and sent off to Cairo, where it took over from the 71st, who were on their way home. The 71st arrived in Scotland to find that their reservists had been recalled to the colours to enable the battalion to keep order at the coal-mines, which it did without any trouble or unpleasantness. It was then in its turn sent to deal with the Irish rebellion, but a truce was signed before the 71st could come to grips with the 'Shinners' which they had been anxious to do, for those gentry were far from popular at the time, even in Ireland.

The 74th, meanwhile, had been sent into Palestine to keep order between the Jews and Arabs. Armed with pick-helves and wicker shields, they 'sorted' both races with a fine impartiality and returned to Cairo where, while polishing themselves up on the eve of the annual Assaye Day parade, they were mobilized and sent off to Chanak in the Dardanelles, at twenty-four hours notice.

The Chanak Expedition of 1922, was dispatched to the Dardanelles in consequence of the re-armament of the Turkish Army, in defiance of the terms of the Armistice, and its attacks on the Greeks and Armenians in Smyrna. Its leader, Mustapha Kemel, then announced his intention of forcing the passage of the Dardanelles and taking Constantinople. The Turkish cavalry arrived on the hills overlooking the Dardanelles just as the 74th landed, but they were driven off by British cavalry without offering any resistance. The 74th then took up a line of outpost positions covering the Narrows, and there remained throughout an exceedingly rough winter, living in bell-tents and bivouacs with the whole land feet deep in snow, while icy winds swept down the coast and the Turks, some sixty thousand strong, marched and counter-marched a few miles inland. The affair was eventually settled without bloodshed through the efforts of the Commander-in-Chief, Sir Charles Harington, and the 74th returned to Cairo just in time to polish themselves up for the Assaye Day parade of 1923. This notable occasion was marred by the absence of Lord Allenby, the Governor-General, owing to the Egyptian assassination of Sir Lee Stack, the Governor-General of the Sudan. Following the murder the 74th spent a good deal of time marching about Cairo and its vicinity at full strength, in order to weaken any intentions the inhabitants might have had of making forceful demonstrations in support of the assassins. The situation consequently quietened down, and the 74th left for India in the following year in a very friendly atmosphere.

A few years of comparative peace and quiet now ensued for both regular battalions of the Highland Light Infantry during which the regiment was granted the additional title of City of Glasgow Regiment, in recognition of its long association with that city, and from which most of its recruits had been obtained. An official affiliation was also concluded with the Highland Light Infantry of Canada, a distinguished regiment of Militia which had originated in 1837, although it did not assume the designation of H.L.I. of Canada until 1920.

After spending some years in the 'garden city' of Bangalore in Mysore State—which their forebears had taken by storm 130 years previously—the 74th changed station to Cawnpore in 1928. Regiments changing station in India still used their feet, as they had always done, marching at the rate of about fifteen miles a day over hundreds of miles of hills and plain, across rivers and through forests; receiving civic receptions at every large township, and with every man greatly enjoying the experience. The 74th on the line of march, headed by the pipes, and with the military band in the centre, was a very fine sight indeed, which was thoroughly enjoyed by the inhabitants of the country traversed, none of whom had any political understanding or nationalist learnings. Affairs in the big industrial city of Cawnpore were however, somewhat different, for it was one of the centres of the Congress Party, headed by Ghandi, which, though it could not be described as anti-British, was continually agitating for 'Dominion Status', which was as far as its political aspirations had reached at that time. The undercurrent of tension which flowed beneath the outwardly placid surface of life in Cawnpore was caused however, not by the Congress Party, which was forever preaching non-violence, but by the racial hatred existing between Hindus and Mohammedans.

The city had a large Scottish community, mostly employed in managing the cotton mills. Inspired by the arrival of the 74th, and learning that the battalion was to act as hosts at a forthcoming athletic gathering of the Highland Brigade, the Scotsmen presented a championship trophy for competition at the Games, but before the gathering took place, riots broke out in the city between the Hindus and Mohammedans which quickly developed into wholesale massacres. The police having lost control, the 74th had to be called in to restore order. Only two companies were in station at the time, but they got the situation in hand within a couple of days without firing a shot. Patrols then continued to be sent out for some time, although, until the hundreds of corpses could be dealt with the stench in the narrow streets was such that the doctors feared the outbreak of an epidemic among the troops.

The Highland Brigade Gathering was eventually held in 1931, with the Black Watch, H.L.I., Seaforth, Gordons and Camerons taking part. The trophy was very appropriately won by the 74th, after a close finish against the Gordons. Their success naturally gave great satisfaction to the Scots in Cawnpore. The battalion also won the Highland Brigade Football League Championship and the Murray Cup Championship for the football teams of regiments stationed in the United Provinces, Bengal and Assam. This particular trophy, like the Durand, had been won by the regiment five times, including 1894 and 1895, the first two years of its existence, for which the trophies are still in the possession of the regiment; for it was not turned into a challenge cup until the H.L.I. had won it twice.

In 1932, the 74th were transferred to Razmak, a great military camp in the mountains along the North-West Frontier. Here they quickly acquired what the Indian Army had turned into the highly specialized art of fighting Pathans; a ponderous business with the emphasis on protection, in order to avoid being surprised. Every height along the flanks of the advance had to be picqueted by troops sent out by the advanced guard; the picquets being drawn in by the rear guard. The Pathans soon learnt the rules, and would endeavour to creep up on the picquets unobserved, ready to rush them as soon as they started to withdraw. Having become adepts at this grisly sort of game, the 74th marched off from Peshawar to the Mohmand Campaign of 1935 with rather more than their usual enthusiasm, and were soon 'playing at long balls' with the Pathans, who showed a strong reluctance to come to close quarters. Two permanent picquets for the protection of the main camp were established and held by the battalion; one of them, by the order of Brigadier Auchenleck, being named Highland Picquet and the other Assaye Picquet. In addition time was found for the H.L.I. monogram and crown to be carved on the rocks alongside the road through the Nahakki Pass. The campaign ended within the year, and the 74th returned to Peshawar, with some half-dozen casualties and a couple of awards for gallantry to show for their experience.

The 71st, after spells in Ireland, Malta and Dover, had, at the end of 1934, been posted to Fort George, which they had last seen in 1881, just before amalgamation with the 74th. The international situation was worsening, owing to the caperings of Mussolini, the Dictator of Italy, who, in 1936, invaded Abyssinia for no reason other than naked conquest. Economic sanctions against Italy were imposed but scornfully evaded, and doubts arose regarding the security of British interests in the Middle East. In Fort George, the officers of the 71st had just arrived at their companies for the first parade, when the bugles rang out *officers at the double*, and, on responding to the call, they were informed, to their great astonishment, that the battalion had been placed under immediate orders for Egypt.

In a very short space of time, the battalion then found itself sharing a tented camp in the desert with the horses of the Light Cavalry Brigade, which had just abandoned its 'long-faced pals' in favour of armoured cars. Also sharing the camp was a vast number of flies, whose attentions the 71st could more cheerfully have endured had there been any indication that the battalion was intended for some useful purpose. No such indication was however, apparent, and having spent the summer in the desert, the 71st returned to Fort George in time to experience the first of the winter gales of snow and sleet which had so disconcerted Prince Charlie's Highlanders on the field of Culloden nearby.

Encouraged by Mussolini's conquest of Abyssinia and successful defiance of the League of Nations the Chancellor of Germany, Adolf Hitler, embarked on a series of invasions against his neighbouring countries in Europe. Conscription or 'National Service', as it was called, was thereupon imposed in Great Britain and the 71st, whose total strength for a number of years had not exceeded 400, were thus brought up to establishment. They were not however, furnished with any modern arms other than the Bren light machine-gun and its carrier. They had no anti-tank weapons and their horses, which were retained up to the eve of war, were not replaced by mechanized transport suitable for the field. For many years, the battalion had dragged about some wooden anti-tank guns made by the Pioneer Sergeant who, as war became imminent, had to turn his hand to the construction of some anti-aircraft guns with which to decorate the ancient ramparts of the Fort in case any German reconnaisance aircraft came over to inspect the defences.

War being declared in September, 1939, the 71st mobilized at Elgin where their forebears, Lord Macleod's Highlanders, had first mustered in 1778. Like Macleod's Highlanders the battalion was independent; not belonging to any military formation, and so crossed over to France as Corps troops with the Second Army Corps. Having marched through pouring rain without any first-line transport—for the ancient trucks issued to it had immediately broken down—it eventually arrived in the neighbourhood of Orchies and being given the role of a pioneer battalion, commenced to dig.

As the rest of the British Expeditionary Force was in much the same condition, and the French Army far worse, it was perhaps fortunate that the Germans made no immediate advance on France, but instead invaded Norway, Holland and Denmark. A British force was despatched in a half-hearted effort to succour Norway. It was chiefly composed of 'Independent Companies', the first of which was provided by the 52nd Lowland Division and included elements of the old 157 (H.L.I.) Infantry Brigade, now made up of the 5th and 6th H.L.I. and the Glasgow Highlanders. The H.L.I. platoon of the Independent Company so formed, was the first of the H.L.I. into action in the Second World War. After operations in deep snow among the northern mountains it attempted—on its own—to prevent a surprise German landing at Hemmesberget where, according to the *Official History*, it was still remembered nine years later, 'as having fought with determination through the streets'. Its survivors had eventually to make their escape by boat.

As had happened in the Great War, the Territorial Divisions of the British Army had to take the field while still very inadequately trained. On their arrival in France therefore, one Territorial battalion in each Brigade was exchanged for a Regular battalion in an attempt to bring up the standard. The commander of the 127th Infantry Brigade of the 42nd Division, Brigadier Sir John Smyth, specially asked for the 71st. He had, he said, 'been through some very sticky times with the 71st H.L.I.', in whose company he had won the V.C. during the Great War. The H.L.I., he told the Commander-in-Chief, Lord Gort, 'grouse more than is the traditional privilege of the British soldier. They are certainly always apt to get into trouble over beer and women if given the opportunity; but—when it comes to fighting, they are worth their weight in gold!' This notion, that the H.L.I. were useful fellows to have on one's side in a battle but otherwise rather a nuisance, was fairly generally held. The fact is, that a large proportion of the men of Glasgow are of Highland or Irish ancestry, and so inherit the liking for a fight for its own sake, be the cause what it may. This characteristic is developed in an environment where the lesson is early learned that it is always advisable to get in the first blow, and a certain toughness is thereby acquired which is not otherwise usual, among the citizens of law-abiding Great Britain. The effect has been greatly exaggerated however, and is off-set in any case by many admirable qualities apart from courage, such as a strong sense of humour and an outstanding loyalty.

The enemy offensive opened during the first week in May, 1940, and the French armies disintegrated before it, obliging the British Expeditionary Forces to withdraw to the sea and embark at Dunkirk. The 71st were heavily engaged during this retirement, first along the Scarpe, then before Lille and Armentieres. While in a rear-guard position at Rexpoede, covering the embarkation, the battalion was surrounded and had to fight its way out, losing three officers and twenty-nine rank and file but giving an extremely good account of itself. 'I was particularly pleased with the H.L.I.,' wrote Sir John Smyth. 'I remembered my words to Gort,

"They'll fight like hell when it does start," and they certainly did.'

After the evacuation of the B.E.F., a 'Second B.E.F.' was hurriedly scraped together and landed at Cherbourg in a forlorn hope of bolstering up the defeated French. In it was the 52nd (Lowland) Division, whose 157th (H.L.I.) Brigade was put into defensive positions near Evreaux, where it was the most advanced of any troops in the 'Second B.E.F.' It was heavily attacked on June 13, and thereafter carried out a fighting withdrawal back to Cherbourg, where it embarked on June 18, being one of the last British formations to do so. The enemy entered the port that same evening.

The German victory in France brought Italy into the war on her side. Italy then embarked on various military adventures in the Middle East, with a view to the establishment of a second Roman Empire. It turned out however, that Mussolini had badly miscalculated in regard to the efficiency of the Italian fighting service, which proved to

Imperial War Museum
Scottish troops in the desert at firing practice, May 1940.

be no match for the British without German assistance. The 74th, who at the outbreak of war were in Palestine, moved to the Sudan at the end of 1940, and subsequently took part in the Eritrean Campaign. Unlike the 71st—and the other regular battalions on home service in 1939—the 74th were up to strength in highly-trained officers and men, most of whom had been under fire, either on the Mohmand Campaign or in brushes with the Arabs which had sometimes developed into quite sharp engagements. The battalion consequently had little difficulty in disposing of large numbers of Italians, although the campaign was not without its hard-fought battles, in which many good officers and men were lost. At Barentu for example, on January 26, 1941, the attack of the 4th Indian Division was led by the 10th Infantry Brigade, to which the 74th belonged. The leading companies of the battalion were heavily enfiladed while carrying out a flanking movement, and one of them was halted. The other, led by Captain Mark Hollis, had to cross some very difficult ground and its platoons lost touch with one another, so that when Hollis arrived at the foot of the hill which was his objective, he had no more than a dozen men behind him. He attacked nevertheless, drove off the enemy and destroyed their artillery observation post, but half his men were dead, and he himself mortally wounded. As the enemy massed for a counter-attack under a heavy barrage, he ordered his Sergeant-Major, McMillan, to leave him and withdraw. McMillan was naturally reluctant to do so, and a hot argument ended in the dying officer writing out the order on one of his visiting cards. When the hill was eventually captured, it was found that the enemy had buried the H.L.I. dead in a neat row, with their officer's grave in front.

The 74th subsequently took part in the decisive victory of Keren, at the end of March, which broke the Italian Army of the North. After capturing the Sanchil Ridge, which ended the battle, the battalion erected a large St.

Andrew Cross on the summit of the main feature. The ancient saltire of Scotland had always been carried by the 74th as a regimental flag, but while the Mohmands would certainly have recognized it, it is doubtful if the Italians did so: but probably none of them looked back anyway. On April 1, the battalion arrived before Asmara, the capital of Eritrea, and marched in with all pipes playing. The port of Massawa still held out, and the 74th led into the attack against it on April 5, when the foremost company captured several times its own number of prisoners and was much embarrassed to know how to deal with them—for the battle still raged, and a halt would have made the company unpopular with those behind. However, the white flags were soon showing over the town, and the 74th came out of action and returned to Asmara, where they received a message from the Brigade Commander in his own hand:

To 2nd Battalion H.L.I. From Brigade Commander.

WELL DONE. Massawa April 7.

After the Eritrean Campaign, the 74th moved first to

Imperial War Museum

The H.L.I. go into action with Bren Carriers and lorry-borne troops, June 1942.

Iraq and then to Cyprus. Meanwhile Sir Archibald Wavell had driven the Italians across the Western Desert and out of Cyrenaica; only to lose such large numbers of his forces in an abortive attempt to support Greece that he was unable to withstand the counter-attack and was driven back again and supplanted by Sir Claude Auchenleck, under whom the 74th had served in the Mohmand Campaign. The battalion joined his Eighth Army, at Sollum in March, 1942, two months before the Germans and Italians, led by General Rommel, a commander of great ability, launched another major offensive which succeeded in breaking through the British 8th Army, and forcing it to retreat to the Egyptian Frontier. The 74th were heavily engaged during this period, notably at the Battle of the Cauldron, when General Ritchie, the commander of the 8th Army, endeavoured to destroy the enemy armoured corps when it was momentarily at a disadvantage. The 74th being opposed to armoured forces in the open desert, had a very hard time of it and were overrun many times, often becoming split up into small parties, which had to escape across the desert and find their way back to headquarters as best they could. Sometimes they could not escape: 'One of the platoon, Private Campbell, was last heard shouting "Withdrawal impossible!" He charged a tank, firing his Bren gun from the hip. Most of these brave men were killed or wounded on the spot.'[1]

Gallant exploits by sub-units or groups of a few men were a feature of this withdrawal; such as that of a section of six men of 'C' Company of the 74th, who had a Bren gun in position near Mersa Matruh to protect a field battery covering a gap in the minefield. Enemy infantry wearing British headgear and carried in captured British trucks were allowed to approach the guns unchallenged, but the H.L.I. section, commanded by a Corporal, detected the ruse as the Germans were dismounting and charged

[1] 5th Indian Division History.

immediately, firing from the hip. They disappeared among the enemy lorries and troops, and were apparently all killed, for they were not seen again. Their resolution gave time for the gunners to open up over open sights, blow up many enemy lorries, and retire unhindered.

After the enemy had been halted before the Egyptian frontier, the 74th were withdrawn from the field and sent to Palestine to train for special duties. The battalion thus missed the Battle of Alamein and the subsequent expulsion of the enemy from North Africa. With some engineer and other supporting units, it had been turned into 'No. 2 Beach Brick', for the purpose of establishing a beach-head in the projected invasion of Sicily. It carried out this operation in due course, but as the enemy retired after firing a few shots, it did not go into action, and its only casualty was the commanding-officer, Colonel Thorburn, who was killed by a sniper. Its subsequent beach-head on the coast of Italy, was established unopposed. The 74th were then trained and re-organized as a mountaineer battalion and as such joined the 2nd S.S. Brigade which landed on the islands off Yugoslavia and expelled the Germans therefrom after a good deal of hard fighting carried out in the shape of various commando-type raids often, in the case of the H.L.I., to the sound of the bagpipes. The battalion ended the war in Greece, where it had the unsavoury task of endeavouring to restore and maintain law and order in Athens and elsewhere, in opposition to the Russian-backed 'Peoples' Liberation Army'.

The H.L.I. battalions during the Second World War amounted to ten, not including the H.L.I. of Canada—a large number of whose officers served with the other H.L.I. battalions—but, before the Allied invasion of Europe several of them had become Motor Battalions and the like, and had lost their regimental identity. First of the H.L.I. into the field on 'D-Day', June 6, 1944, was the H.L.I. of Canada, who landed at Berniere-sur-Mer and fought their

General Sir Miles Dempsey presents Colours to the H.L.I., July 1943.

way inland to the Bayeaux-Caen Road. They were followed
on June 13 by the 2nd Glasgow Highlanders in the 46th
Brigade and the 10th H.L.I. in the 227th Brigade of the
15th Scottish Division. Both of these battalions lost heavily
in hard fighting along the Odon river. The 71st, in the 71st
Brigade of the 53rd Welsh Division, arrived in the field on
June 28 and also went into action on the Odon. Unlike the

The 10th H.L.I. move up to the Battle area, June 1944, in Normandy.

situation during the First World War, the Territorial Army had had, by 1944, three years of hard and concentrated training, and its infantry battalions were therefore able to avoid excessive casualties and to prove themselves more than a match for the best the enemy could send against them. There was, furthermore, an abundance of trained Staff Officers, for the Regular Army had not been obliterated during the first year of war, as had happened in 1914, so that the extremely complicated planning necessary for the initial landing in Normandy, and the subsequent operations, was carried out with scarcely a hitch.

While the 71st, Glasgow Highlanders and 10th H.L.I. were fighting their way to the Seine, the Canadians on the left were clearing the Pas de Calais; the H.L.I. of Canada capturing the last of the long-range guns at Cap Grisnez. They sent the Nazi flag and garrison commander's sword to the Mayor of Dover, with the message 'Greetings from the Brigade and may you enjoy your pint of beer and stroll on the front in peace from now on. We have all Jerry's Big Berthas'. At about the same time the 71st arrived in Antwerp and the Glasgow Highlanders at Ghent, where they had a very stiff fight during which one of their men, Private Evans, although mortally wounded fought off a German attack single-handed, and was found dead at his post with ten enemy dead in front of him.

The 6th H.L.I. arrived late into the field owing to the fact that the 52nd Lowland Division, to which it belonged, was being trained as an Airportable Division, in order to support the Airborne Corps in an attack on Arnhem, with the object of seizing the water obstacles in the path of the 21st Army Group. The 1st Airborne Division having failed in a gallant attempt on the Arnhem bridge, the venture was abandoned and the 52nd Division returned to an infantry role. The 6th H.L.I. first joined the 71st in the 71st Infantry Brigade and went into action at Halderen, but on the later arrival of the 157th (H.L.I.) Brigade, it rejoined the 5th H.L.I. and 1st Glasgow Highlanders on the Maas. There were now six H.L.I. battalions in the field, not including the H.L.I. of Canada.

In order to open the port of Antwerp to Allied shipping, it became necessary to occupy the island of Walcheren. Conditions in the Scheldt Estuary had not greatly changed since Napoleon's day, when the 71st visited this insalubrious area in 1809. In 1944 however, the British troops were magnificently trained and equipped, and had the enemy on the run, so that the Walcheren expedition of the year did not come to the same ingominious end as that of 1809. The 5th and 6th H.L.I., the Glagow Highlanders and the H.L.I. of Canada all took part in the assault on Walcheren, where the German garrisons put up a most desperate resistance. Owing to the soft and often waterlogged ground, the deployment of guns and armour was often impracticable, so that the main effort had to be made by the infantry who were however, well-supported by the Royal Navy and R.A.F. Probably the hardest fighting was that for possession of the Walcheren Causeway, linking the island with South Beveland. It was taken by assault by two Canadian regiments which were almost wiped out in the process, so that the 1st Glasgow Highlanders and 6th H.L.I. which followed were hard put to it to maintain the bridgehead. Then, after a crossing had been effected lower down the channel, in which the 5th H.L.I. took part, the enemy resistance weakened and all German garrisons on the island capitulated in turn.

In an effort to interrupt the British operations on the Scheldt, the Germans launched a spoiling attack near Meijel, which overwhelmed the U.S. 7th Armoured Division, and for a while carried everything before it. At the time, the 71st and 1st Glasgow Highlanders were in action at s'Hertogenbosch, while the 10th H.L.I. was in position astride the Meijel road. All three battalions took part in the counter-offensive, before which the enemy withdrew defeated.

In December, 1944, the Germans made a final effort to halt the Allied advance by suddenly launching a major offensive which penetrated the American front to a depth of twenty miles, and placed Brussels itself in danger. It resulted however, in the formation of vulnerable enemy salients in Holland and the Ardennes, which were wiped out by Allied counter-offensives in January, 1945. The 5th and 6th H.L.I. were both in action on the Roer; the latter attacking the village of Bocket, led by its Bren carriers, in one of which the sight of a naked woman standing on the front seat surprised both friend and foe. It turned out to be a dummy model purloined from a dress shop. The 1st

Glasgow Highlanders also took part in these operations, capturing several villages at small cost.

All H.L.I. battalions took part in the subsequent operations, during which the Germans were driven back across the Rhine. Heavy rain had so inundated the battlefield that the H.L.I. of Canada had to go into action afloat in amphibious vehicles, which probably saved them many casualties from mines. A particularly fine performance was put up by the 10th H.L.I. in an attack on Kranenburg, which was very heavily defended being, in fact, one of the bastions of the 'Seigfried Line'. It was taken by the battalion at a cost of three officers and twenty-eight rank and file in killed and wounded. Strange as it may seem however, the modern

Imperial War Museum

October 1944. Near Tilburg men of the 10th H.L.I. on the move. Behind them are the 6th Guard's tanks.

defences of the Seigfried Line did not give the H.L.I. nearly as much trouble as the mediaeval castles of Blijenbeek and Moyland, which their ancestors of the days of Badajoz and Ciudad Rodrigo could probably have taken by storm with little difficulty. The former held out until nine 1,000 lb. bombs had been dropped on it, and the latter had the Glasgow Highlanders completely at a loss, but the general advance fortunately rendered it unnecessary for them to swim the moats and try their hands with scaling ladders.

The crossing of the Rhine, which was carried out on March 23, 1945, was led by the 15th (Scottish) and 51st (Highland) Divisions, with the 10th H.L.I. and 2nd Glasgow Highlanders serving in the former, and the H.L.I. of Canada with the latter, attached to the 154th Brigade. In three days of heavy fighting the H.L.I. of Canada suffered severe casualties during the capture of Bienen and Speldrop, while the 10th H.L.I. captured three villages and 200 prisoners, in securing a bridgehead for the 15th Division: 'In this bitter fight, in which they met and worsted a complete parachute battalion which was fighting with all its accustomed courage, the 10th H.L.I. lost three officers killed and four wounded, fourteen other ranks killed and seventy wounded. They had good reason to look back with pride on their Rhine crossing.'[1] The quickstep *The 10th H.L.I. crossing the Rhine* was composed by Pipe-Major Donald Shaw Ramsay, in honour of the occasion.

The parachute battalion concerned belonged to the 7th German Parachute Division, other units of which were encountered by the 2nd Glasgow Highlanders and 6th H.L.I., which had crossed the Rhine in the lead of the 52nd (Lowland) Division. The German parachutists were renowned for their fighting spirit, but it proved quite unequal to that of their opponents, and after resisting fiercely for a while they began to give up, so that as the 6th H.L.I. swept through the woods they met no resistance.

[1] 15th Division History.

White flags were flying everywhere, and large numbers of exhausted and dispirited prisoners were taken. Beyond Osnabruck however, the 6th H.L.I. came up against the officer cadets and their instructors from the German military schools, who were expert soldiers with a spirit to match. Armed only with rifles, they held up not only the 6th H.L.I. but the whole Brigade; causing heavy casualties before they could be driven off. This in fact, was not achieved until the 71st Brigade of the Welsh Division arrived, with the 71st H.L.I. in the lead, supported by three artillery regiments and a number of tanks and flame-throwers.

With the German Army disintegrating in front of it, the 21st Army Group advanced with extraordinary rapidity; many infantry units riding forward on tanks. Normal formations could not be adhered to under such circumstances, and some odd encounter battles took place. Near Uelzen, for instance, the 10th H.L.I. hurtling along forest tracks on the tanks of the Scots Guards, were flung into action piecemeal, when the column ran into an ambush. It was some time before the officers were able to get the battle organized, but the soldiers seem to have been quite happy banging away at the Germans on their own. Uelzen itself was defended by Panzer Grenadiers, who were fresh troops of the highest quality and held out to the end against the two Brigades of the 15th (Scottish) Division sent against them. In the initial stages the 10th H.L.I. got half-way through the suburbs after desperate hand-to-hand fighting through the streets, during which they took 400 prisoners. The 2nd Glasgow Highlanders came in at the end, clearing each house in Uelzen with the bayonet during the final assault, when it took two Brigades eleven hours to finish off the Grenadiers, by which time most of the town was on fire.

After all Germans had been cleared out by Holland by the Canadians, and the British troops had taken Bremen and Hamburg, the enemy high command surrendered on May

Field Marshal Montgomery decorates Sgt. R. Campbell, 10th H.L.I. with the M.M.

4, 1945. All H.L.I. battalions were in the front line to the end. The 71st were at Hamburg, and almost as soon as the cease-fire was sounded in the west, were placed under orders for the east, where the Japanese were still in the field, although at the end of their tether. Their surrender after the dropping of the atomic bomb in August, resulted in the 71st going no further east than Jerusalem.

In the Second World War, the Highland Light Infantry lost in dead 104 officers and 1,287 rank and file; not including the H.L.I. of Canada who lost twenty-four officers and 294 rank and file. Good training and the use of all manner of novel supporting weapons had kept the casualties at a reasonable figure in spite of all the hard fighting; but there were of course, a considerable number of wounded who owed their lives to new medical skills and the efficiency of the arrangements for dealing with casualties.

The regiment won 215 decorations for gallantry; apart

from thirty-eight gained by the H.L.I. of Canada. Although there were many individual deeds of heroism, only one was held to merit a Victoria Cross, which was awarded posthumously to Major F. G. Blaker, for his conduct while leading a company of the 9th Gurkha Rifles, to whom he was attached, against a Japanese position in Burma.

Chapter
8

Conclusion

IN 1947, the kilt was restored to the Highland Light Infantry, and its T.A. battalions were transferred from the 52nd (Lowland) Division to the 51st (Highland) Division. The anomalous position in which the regiment found itself after reorganization of the Army in 1881 was therefore at last removed. In the same year, H.R.H. The Princess Margaret was appointed Colonel-in-Chief, in succession to her great grand-uncle, Field-Marshal H.R.H. The Duke of Connaught and Strathearn, who had died in 1942. A year later, at a ceremony in Glasgow, H.R.H. the Colonel-in-Chief received on behalf of the Highland Light Infantry 'the Freedom of Entry into the City and Royal Burgh of Glasgow on ceremonial occasions with bayonets fixed, drums beating and colours flying'.

The official recognition of the Highland traditions of the regiment, and the honour conferred by His Majesty by the appointments of another royal Colonel-in-Chief; followed by the Freedom of the City of Glasgow, were naturally contemplated with great pride and satisfaction by all soldiers of the H.L.I. past and present, as being rewards well-earned by the services of the regiment in two world wars at the cost of well over 11,000 lives. 170 years had passed since Lord Macleod had first raised his Highlanders who had fought with such distinction all over the world, and there seemed no reason to doubt that as long a period lay ahead, during which the H.L.I. could be counted upon to maintain the proud heritage handed down to them. Under such circumstances the disappearance of the 74th which, in common with all second battalions, had been placed 'in suspended animation', was regarded without undue dismay, especially as it was hoped that the old regiment had not disappeared for good. The Assaye Colour was therefore carried by the 71st, until such time as a resuscitated 74th could claim it back again.

There were however, ominous indications of a general retirement from all British overseas possessions and spheres of influence. In Egypt the flag which had been hoisted over the Citadel in Cairo by the 74th in 1882 was, by a curious chance, hauled down again by the 71st in 1946. The 71st had suffered some eighty casualties in Palestine while trying to keep order among the Jews and Arabs, and had been sent to Egypt for a 'rest'. This lengthened to two years, spent in detachments along the Canal Zone, during which the battalion won practically every sporting event possible. It then returned to Jerusalem to find the Holy Land in chaos. In the middle of Jerusalem itself, sixteen soldiers were shot while peaceably drinking tea in a cafe, in spite of the fact that the Jewish murderers were dependent on the H.L.I. for escorting their food supplies through the Arab cordon round the Old City. However, the British flag was hauled down over Jerusalem in May, 1948, and the 71st came home to Scotland and quartered at Fort George. In 1950, the battalion was suddenly bundled into aircraft and dumped down in the desert near Tobruk, without being given any reason for the trip. After five months it was transferred to Malta, and in 1952 back to the Canal Zone. Here, like all other of the unfortunate British regiments along the Suez Canal, they had to endure constant attacks from Egyptian ruffians without being allowed to reply to them; subsequently burying their murdered comrades in the cemetery at Tel-el-Kebir, to rest alongside those of the 74th killed in action against Arabi Pasha in 1882.

The Canal Zone having been evacuated in 1954, the 71st returned to the United Kingdom, where they just had time to receive new colours from H.R.H. the Colonel-in-Chief before being stood-to once more and flown out to Cyprus, where numbers of the Greek population had commenced guerrilla operations against the British authorities, with the aim of getting the island taken over by Greece—an idea which was very unpopular with the Turkish inhabitants. The 71st were thus again plunged into the middle of a sordid struggle which could have only the one end—British policy being what it was. The battalion spent just over a year in the island, before joining the British Army of the Rhine in 1957. On leaving Cyprus, they were complimented by the Governor, Field-Marshal Sir John Harding, who said '. . . you have got your area in that settled state we would like to see in the rest of Cyprus. You have had a great variety of tasks to perform; some of them have been tedious, difficult and dangerous, and you have taken them all in the spirit that I would expect from your Regiment. You have had casualties, but you have taken the rough with the smooth. Well done. Well done, the Highland Light Infantry.' The battalion was fortunate, in that during twelve months of encounters with the Greek guerrillas it lost only three men killed, who were murdered in cold blood while watching a company football match.

The dissolution of the British Empire, having led to a considerable reduction in British military commitments overseas, conscription, or National Service, as it was called, was ended in 1957, and plans made for re-organizing the British Army on a reduced scale. The intention was to avoid the disbandment of regiments by amalgamating certain of them with others, with the idea that the new regiments so formed would be in a legitimate position to inherit and maintain the traditions of the old regiments from which they sprang. The regiments selected for amalgamation, in general, accepted their fate with philosophic resignation; the two exceptions being the Highland Light Infantry and the Royal Scots Fusiliers which, one being Highland and the other Lowland, were unable to contemplate with any degree of equanimity what appeared to be the virtually impossible task of merging their entirely different identities. These grounds of objection were however, not understood south of the border.

It had been announced, that regiments objecting to amalgamation would be permitted to volunteer for disbandment, but when, after obtaining the opinions of the past and present members of their regiments, the Colonels of the Highland Light Infantry and Royal Scots Fusiliers declared their preference for disbandment, their resignations were called for and the amalgamation ordered to be carried out.

In consequence, the separate history of the Highland Light Infantry came to an end at the beginning of 1959, after a period of service lasting 180 years, during which few battles were fought against the enemies of the United Kingdom without the stout participation of the regiment, whose history is, in effect, that of the rise and fall of the British Empire.

It must be said in conclusion, that, however offensive the prospect of amalgamation seemed to them at the time, the Highland Light Infantry and Royal Scots Fusiliers had so much to offer one another that the result, in the formation of the Royal Highland Fusiliers, has produced a regiment of rare quality, which has already made something of a mark both at home and abroad. It can certainly be counted upon to display the characteristics on the battlefield of the 21st, 71st and 74th regiments, in any dispute which the United Kingdom may in the future be obliged to settle by force of arms.

The Highland Light Infantry

1777-1959

1777	73rd (Lord Macleod's) Highlanders raised.
1778	2nd Battalion of the 73rd raised.
1780—83	1/73rd in Southern India. Fought at Conjeveram, Porto Novo, Sholinghur, Vellore, Cuddalore and Arcot.
	2/73rd as marines in Rodney's fleet at the 'Moonlight Battle' off Cape St. Vincent, and in the Siege of Gibraltar. Battalion disbanded 1783.
1786	73rd re-numbered 71st.
1786—97	71st at sieges of Bangalore and Seringapatam.
1787	74th Highlanders raised by Sir Archibald Campbell of Inverneil.
1799	74th at the storming and capture of Seringapatam.
1803	74th awarded a Third Colour in recognition of their conduct at the Battle of Assaye.
1806	71st at the capture of the Cape of Good Hope.
1807	71st at the capture of Buenos Ayres.
1808—09	71st in the battles of Roleia, Vimiera and Corunna.
1808	71st with the Walcheren Expedition and at the siege and capture of Flushing. Made a Light Infantry Regiment and thereafter known as the 71st Highland Light Infantry.
1810—14	71st and 74th in the Peninsula War. Fought at Busaco, Fuentes D'Onor, Almaraz, Badajoz, Ciudad Rodrigo, Salamanca, Vittoria, Arinez, Pyrenees, Nive, Nivelle, Orthes, Toulouse.

1815   71st at the Battle of Waterloo.

1838   71st assist in quelling a rebellion in Canada.

1851—53   74th in the Kaffir War. Sinking of the *Birkenhead*.

1855—56   71st in the Crimea War.

1858—59   71st in the Central India Campaign.

1863   71st in the Ambeyla Campaign.

1881   71st and 74th linked to become the 1st and 2nd Battalions of the Highland Light Infantry.

1881—83   2nd H.L.I. in the Egyptian Campaign and at the Battle of Tel-el-Kebir.

1898   1st H.L.I. in the insurrection in Crete.

1899—1902   1st H.L.I. in the South African War.

1900—42   Field-Marshal H.R.H. The Duke of Connaught and Strathearn, Colonel-in-Chief.

1897—98   74th in the Malakand Campaign.

1908   3rd and 4th (Special Reserve) 5th, 6th, 7th, 8th and 9th (Glasgow Highlanders) Territorial Army Battalions, H.L.I. formed.

1914—18   First World War. H.L.I. battalions increased to twenty-six, fighting in France, Belgium, Dardanelles, Egypt, Palestine and Mesopotamia. Losses in dead: 598 officers, 9,428 rank and file.

1919   2nd H.L.I. in the Expedition to North Russia.

1920   29th Waterloo Battalion of Canadian Militia re-named the H.L.I. of Canada.

1922—23   2nd H.L.I. in the Chanak Expedition.

1923   H.L.I. becomes the City of Glasgow Regiment. H.L.I. of Canada affiliated.

1931   2nd H.L.I. quell the Cawnpore Riots.

1935   2nd H.L.I. in the Mohmand Campaign.

1939—45   Second World War. H.L.I. battalions fought in Normandy, France, Belgium, Holland, Germany, Western Desert, Sudan, Eritrea,

	Iraq, Libya, Cyrenaica, Sicily and Italy, and in the islands off Yugoslavia.
1946	2nd H.L.I. in Greece and Salonica.
1947—59	H.R.H. The Princess Margaret, Colonel-in-Chief.
1947	2nd H.L.I. placed 'in suspended animation'.
1946—48	1st H.L.I. in Egypt and Palestine.
1956	1st H.L.I. in Cyprus.
1959	The Highland Light Infantry amalgamated with the Royal Scots Fusiliers to form the Royal Highland Fusiliers.